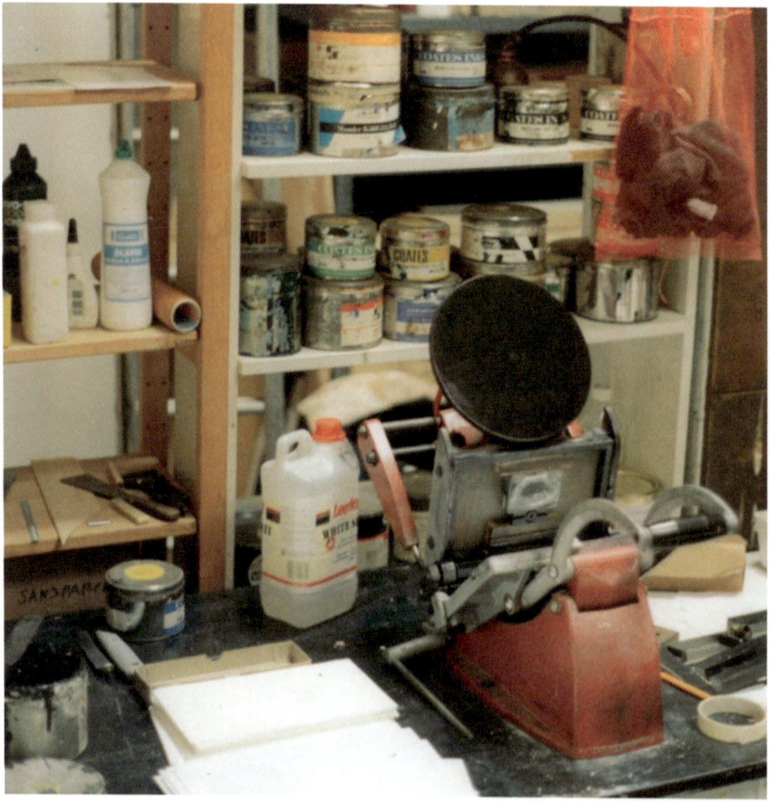

Printed in Norfolk

Coracle Publications 1989–2012

RGAP 2012

THE GALLERY
Norwich University College of the Arts
St George's Street, Norwich NR3 1BB
20 March–21 April 2012

SHANDY HALL
Coxwold, York YO61 4AD
15 September–14 October 2012

SAISON POETRY LIBRARY
Royal Festival Hall, London SE1 8XX
1–30 November 2012

With financial support from The Elephant Trust, The Henry Moore Foundation, the National Lottery through Arts Council England, Norfolk County Council

ISBN 978-0-9569024-1-2
Designed by Colin Sackett
Printed and bound in the U.K.

RGAP
(Research Group for Artists Publications)
Yorkshire Artspace
21 Brown Street, Sheffield S1 2BS
www.rgap.co.uk

Distributed by
Cornerhouse Publications
70 Oxford Street, Manchester M1 5NH
www.cornerhouse.org

Don't ever be intimidated by the disdain or disinterest in the world. Get yourself some type, get yourself some paper, and print it.

CHARLES OLSON

Foreword

Coracle is a one-word poem, the title of which is a reading in and of the places it moves through.

The activities of Coracle have been important for over thirty years because it has encouraged the book—both in terms of manufacture and reception (printing and stitching as much as turning a page and reading)—to be understood to issue forth and stand as a tangible space, a platform, for critical activity. The place of reading, and the recognition of that as a locality, is at the heart of much that Coracle does. From a specific place, always in relation to local resources and particularities, Coracle recognises that, even though fleet of foot, the place of making and reading underpins meaning and affect. Production is not fetishised (in terms of the artist's book as form or material), but is determined by function—reading and looking as a critical activity carried out with a book in the hand.

This simple principle has informed the spaces within which Coracle has existed since 1975—in London, Liverpool, Norfolk, Italy or Ireland. The model may well be that of the Little Magazine—a magazine produced usually as a result of avant-garde urgency and few resources to communicate ideas to a small (but perhaps far-flung) community—but the means is the small press, being not just the printing press itself, but the space it sits in and its relationship to other areas of making and reading and looking. Prior to Coracle, Simon Cutts had been involved in Tarasque Press that produced an eponymous magazine in this way and also, significantly, had a base in a book space, the Trent Bookshop. Apart from the very occasional *Little Critic*, Coracle has not produced a magazine, one reason perhaps being that its whole production and activity mirrors to an extent that of a Little Magazine; printed by a small press in a sequence of specific places.

ANDREW WILSON

Contents

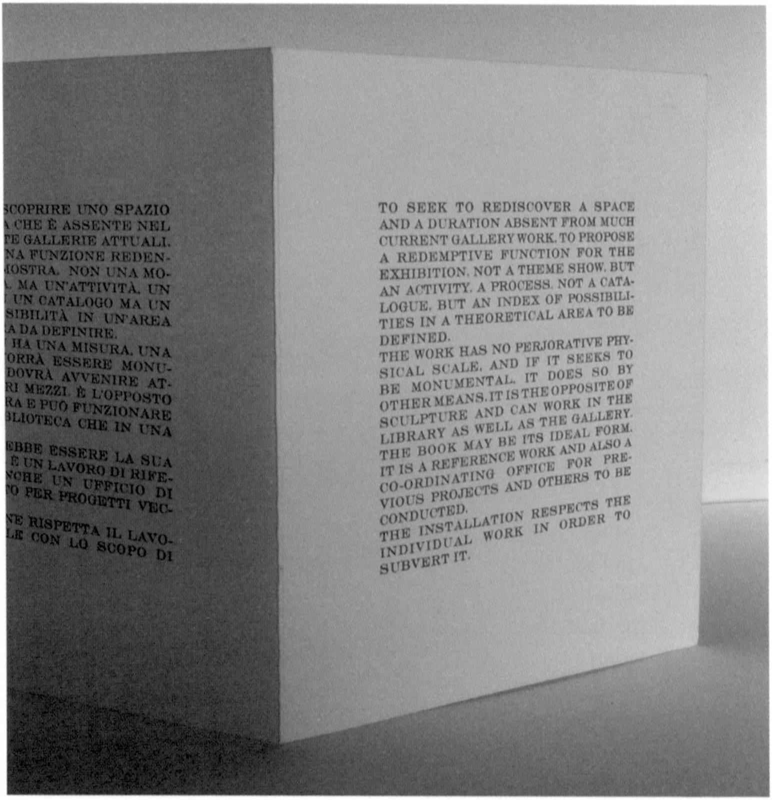
TO SEEK TO REDISCOVER A SPACE AND A DURATION ABSENT FROM MUCH CURRENT GALLERY WORK. TO PROPOSE A REDEMPTIVE FUNCTION FOR THE EXHIBITION. NOT A THEME SHOW, BUT AN ACTIVITY. A PROCESS. NOT A CATALOGUE, BUT AN INDEX OF POSSIBILITIES IN A THEORETICAL AREA TO BE DEFINED.
THE WORK HAS NO PERJORATIVE PHYSICAL SCALE, AND IF IT SEEKS TO BE MONUMENTAL, IT DOES SO BY OTHER MEANS. IT IS THE OPPOSITE OF SCULPTURE AND CAN WORK IN THE LIBRARY AS WELL AS THE GALLERY.
THE BOOK MAY BE ITS IDEAL FORM. IT IS A REFERENCE WORK AND ALSO A CO-ORDINATING OFFICE FOR PREVIOUS PROJECTS AND OTHERS TO BE CONDUCTED.
THE INSTALLATION RESPECTS THE INDIVIDUAL WORK IN ORDER TO SUBVERT IT.

SIMON CUTTS

The Norfolk Years

I remember the distinct urge to return to our books and publications full-time whilst sitting in the huge gallery in Florence, in all its edifying space and calm. There was a splendid accompanying bookroom, but it was not enough to appease the sensation. It was towards the autumn of 1990, and in spite of several highly eclectic exhibitions we had done there, the impulse would not go away even while I was dealing with the arrangement of a space, a given space that I grew to know and to alter like the pages of a book. I was trying to find a way to make an exhibition with the poet Robert Lax living in Greece, amongst other things, and the apex of that summer had been the making of Rüdiger Schöttle's *Stadt Aus Glas,* the small houses for which were made by local glass craftsmen. They were covered in ultra-violet powder, the lights were left on, and we quit for the summer. It glowed from across the river. When we returned, we installed the refrigeration units of Paul Etienne Lincoln's *New York Hot, New York Cold,* each of which made $5 bonds of ice, and produced a small catalogue of facsimiles of them. But in the context surrounding such galleries, or at least this gallery, books and publications were seen as mere hand-outs, to be given to collectors, maybe as a prompt to buy something bigger. One collector I knew at the time, shrink-wrapped everything he was given, so that he couldn't see what was inside!

So it was time to reconsider. By the very early part of 1991, we had returned to our small house in Norfolk, and our warehouse down the road, as the main base of our activities. Back in the summer of 1984, I had written in the foreword to the touring exhibition catalogue for *The Unpainted Landscape*:

> …I laboured with a spade about my house and garden in Norfolk and on the title for the exhibition. That which emerged still gives me much pleasure. This book, as ever for Coracle, is pivotal to the exhibition…

This present exhibition and its catalogue *Printed in Norfolk: Coracle Publications 1989–2012*, arose as a sort of caprice thrown up by Erica Van Horn on the demise of our favourite printers—Crome & Akers in Kings Lynn—at the end of 2010: shouldn't we celebrate what we had done with them, and while doing it, include our book-binder friend Stuart Settle nearby in Fakenham? There was a fitting localness to it all, and although it may not provide a complete bibliography of the later phase of Coracle production, it would be copious and, we hoped, a little didactic, a way of seeing what you can do within limited means. Helen Mitchell in Norwich took on the idea as an organisational challenge. Martin Rogers of the Research Group for Artists Publications agreed to have it under his umbrella, and facilitate the tour of the exhibition and publish the catalogue, and when it was first listed in the calendar for The Gallery at Norwich University College of the Arts, I knew it had been rooted as an idea, and we should get on and put it together. We might improvise a little within the parameters of the title.

Coracle is one of a handful of small presses emerging from the nineteen fifties and sixties in Britain, Ireland and America, continuing to build the platform of publishing and publication as a project for primary work. They often arose out of the need to make new writing and criticism available in the form of the little magazine and the poetry primer, and to establish their presence. To some extent these presses from that time, often run by artists and poets, remain a model of activity in this field. A more formal bibliography of the latter part of Coracle is needed. It may well happen in due course. By a long-term arrangement the Coracle Papers are kept at the Getty Research Institute in California, a long way from all this. The Yale Center for British Art in New Haven, Connecticut had made the large retrospective and bibliography of the first half of Coracle in 1989, under the auspices of Duncan Robinson, then director. The library at The British Art Center has now moved focus almost exclusively to the white-glove treatment of books (ametaphorical cut-out paper butterflies in glass boxes). They disregard distribution and availability, no matter how hypothetical—and this has always been the main tenet of Coracle, in favour of the rareity of collection. I had written in *Spines & Spirals: The Norfolk Books 1990-1996*:

> Coracle books seek the *generality* of the occasion for a publication, which may arise from its *particularity*: the observation and recording of a phenomenon, the identification of genres, the seemingly obsessive classification. In this they may resemble less other artists' books, whatever they are, than *all* books in general, surveyed eclectically.
>
> It is indeed by now difficult to substantiate any single definition of a book made by an artist, and this very issue may well have already been surpassed. There are *only* books in an intensified and eclectic arena. Often these books subvert the notion of illustration, of separate parts of text and image, which may belong to the earlier considerations of the *private* presses, and more predicated on rarity and luxury. These new books attempt to synthesise text, image, material, method of production, and context, into a unified single work. If this succeeds the book functions as a primary form.

The uncanny parallels between the earlier phase of Coracle, and that of the situation in Norfolk are taken up by John Bevis in his essay 'A Star-gazey Pie', but I think I could elaborate a little further on some of them. The use of two almost identical printers, by way of Edward Wells & Sons in Camberwell New Road, London, and Crome & Akers in Austin Street, Kings Lynn, Norfolk is remarkable. They were both small family firms with successive generations entering the trade. They both had letterpress and offset printing, and both produced in the main vernacular jobs for the locality—raffle and club tickets, cattle-market posters, and all manner of stationery for weddings and funerals. In the Camberwell years of Coracle, we had learned to work locally, and the impetus to use what was around us arose simply from a desire to see what could be done with what they could do. In the seventies and eighties we had used the whole manufacturing base of the nearby districts of London, the box-makers, block-makers, paper merchants and engravers, makers of cutters, creasers and die-formes that could be stamped in the press. Now it seems as if this whole manufacturing base has disappeared. We are left with trying to get tactility of some sort from an implacable electronic screen.

Sometime in 1989 I walked into Crome & Akers, Kings Lynn, with the idea of trying something in a new town, and armed with a notebook notion of my *Nine Poems*, to enquire if we could get differing coloured slugs of type to drop onto a plain page. The final job was almost faultless. It was quickly followed by Erica Van Horn's *Jewels I Have Loved*, where single coloured words are dropped into the black text, a procedure I had dreamed of since the days of the small treadle platen under the stairs at the Trent Bookshop. These were quickly followed by the pamphlet *Palpa* with its linotype setting and thermographed pink blotting paper cover. Such materials were supplemented by plain coloured manilla file-index board and materials the Cromes found in their dusty storeroom. The covering paper of the ledger bindings of *The Rubber Stamp Mini-Printer Series* from 1993 and 1995 are receipt-book papers from the nineteenth century. During the Norfolk years, the books and other printed objects tried to achieve an idiomatic plainness, a simplicity and generality of form and content, perhaps almost parallel in development to the genre of the artist's book.

The books were also warehoused and packed in Docking, Norfolk, and supplied to bookshops and libraries throughout Europe, America and latterly Japan. This distribution was often the result of visits to such places, to particular libraries and collections, or the follow-up to showing the books at trade fairs like The Frankfurt Book Fair during this period. The issue of a bookshop as a means of distribution has always been of central concern to Coracle, and with the beginning of *workfortheeyetodo* in London in the mid-nineties, the need for print and paper as a means of announcement, for reminder, and for the burlesque of a venue. As it had been in the Camberwell days, this occupied a good part of the ephemera of the time, with the postcard as ever the main vehicle.

The main difference between these two periods in practical terms is that in Norfolk we developed our relationship with a single book-binder, Stuart Settle in Oxwick, near Fakenham. In the London years, there were a variety of trade binders we used depending on the particularities of a job. In Stuart we had found a trade bookbinder who did our jobs in his shed in his spare time, and who could adapt to the solving of problems as they arose from our strange demands. Sometimes the book-blocks would be collated and sewn by Kayleigh Print Finishers in Fakenham and transferred to Stuart for casing and blocking. But imagine being confronted by a book-block of plain red paper which needed drilling through with a hole that connected to the centre of a spiral blocked on the front and back of a red case cover. This was the production of Yoko Terauchi's *coil / join*. There was no other content to the book, beyond the paper and his binding.

Stuart was a master of case binding, having trained at night-school in Norwich as an apprentice tradesman, and together with him we developed the archetypal plain book, a platonic bookness, almost a memory of the first book. He had also inherited a vast supply of rolls of coloured bookcloth from Fakenham Press when it closed. It was the trade idioms of both printing and binding that we wanted to harness, and to shift slightly towards the critical content of each book: the seemingly automatic layout of the letterpress chase forme, allied to the economics of paper folding, and the austerity of the simple case binding. Eventually with Stuart we began to use even the foil-blocking of the covers as a print device, but far from the over-elaborate 'craft' of tooling and embossing of the society of Designer Bookbinders.

Even when we moved to Ireland in the late nineties, we continued to produce, print and bind in Norfolk, and sometimes finish on the Adana now in its shed in Ireland. Amongst the first jobs to be done was a change of address card, citing and siting two concrete addresses which no postman has ever really taken seriously.

CORACLE	CORACLE
DOCKING	BALLYBEG
NORFOLK	GRANGE
ENGLAND	CLONMEL
PE31 8LQ	TIPPERARY
	IRELAND

JOHN BEVIS

A Star-gazey Pie[1]

It's very Coracle. Not Coraclesque, or Coraclist, or Coraclean, simply *Coracle.* It's very *Coracle.*

It's an epithet that, like a freemason's cipher, can inform or mystify depending on who is listening. What does it mean, for example, in the context of an exhibition title such as *Foto Cliché*, or *Schaufelbagger und Muldenkipper*, or *The Unpainted Landscape*; or catalogues in the shape of boxed cigarette cards and luggage labels? What about the postcard of a sign seen on a newsagent's stand, 'PROLONGED READING NOT APPRECIATED'? Or the transformation of a Camberwell shop into the subject of an Edward Hopper painting? What about invitation 'cards' in the form of coat hangers, pieces of trellis and MDF, rain hats and plastic spades? For each of these somebody, somewhere, at some time, has reached for an adjective and grasped *Coracle.*

Aside from an underplayed wit, it's not obvious what the common denominator is; what it is that makes these *Coracle* and not *Courtauld* or *Cornerhouse* or *Corsham.* To begin to understand *Coracle* is to know something of Coracle, which was responsible for the items listed above. A small press for artists' books, objects, poetry and criticism, it commenced operations as Coracle Press in 1975. For eleven years from 1976 it fronted production under the banner Coracle Press Books & Gallery; later phases introduced Coracle Docking, in Norfolk; Coracle Atlantic, in Liverpool; and Coracle Distribution, encompassing bookshops in Cambridge and Whitechapel. For one period the venture went incognito as workfortheeyetodo; for another, a parcel of its identity was blurred in the operations management of the Victoria Miro Gallery. At some point along the way it settled into the guise of its own street name, plain Coracle, where it remains.

Throughout, it has been the *nom de chapeau* of Simon Cutts, artist and poet, printer and publisher, bookseller and curator, working at different times—or simultaneously—alone, in partnerships, in collectives of any number from two up, and within collaborations and commissions. Under his stewardship, the two Coracles—roman and italic—have twisted their double helix together into an inseparable whole, the DNA of a remarkable life in art and publishing.

Mixed Media Hazard [2]

Take a hammer
and make
your autobiography

Coracle, the name, is of course a one man boat, an apparatus for travelling light, a home-made affair, vessel of waterways unexplored and inaccessible, and symbol of crafts ancient and quaint. In reality Coracle, the venture, outgrew all of these sentiments in a short time. It was from the start too gregarious, too encompassing. But any perspective on where it stands, and what it stands for, is made more difficult by the way it has overwhelmed conventions to have been both commercial and anti-commercial, shoestring and corporate, shopfront and backroom, its aim set sometimes into and sometimes outwith the proverbial tent.

The résumé of Coracle operations suggests that some essential constants are to be found, paradoxically, in variety. Writing, printing, publishing, bookshops, galleries, curating, archiving and warehousing fall within its ministry. But if Simon Cutts is no small-press Robert Maxwell, neither is Coracle unique in being a mansion of many chambers; what is distinctive is the culture of bartering and buttressing between its parts, enabled by a blindness to the mental barriers separating structure, media, methods and materials. The result is a more than usually sovereign organisation, powered by its own internal combustion. As Simon Cutts said of learning letterpress printing: "the expertise provoked the work itself."[3]

The progress of Coracle has been, like any other

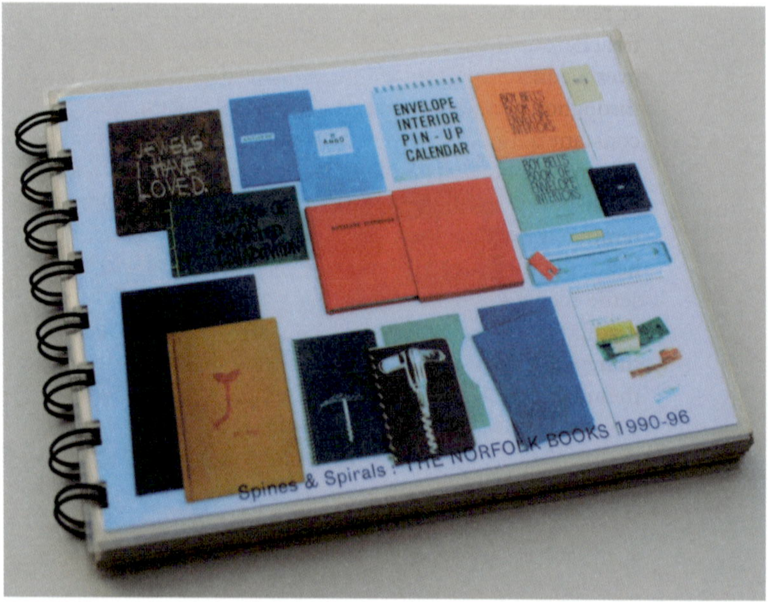
JEWELS I HAVE LOVED.
ENVELOPE
INTERIOR
PIN - UP
CALENDAR
BOY BELL'S BOOK OF ENVELOPE INTERIORS
Spines & Spirals : THE NORFOLK BOOKS 1990-96

evolution, a mix of startling novelties, linear developments, abrupt redirections, false starts and forgetfulness. At times the changes have been radical enough to imply the negation or rejection of what has gone before, to seem almost treacherous. This has, inevitably, thrown a smokescreen over a consistency of attitude and practice sustained throughout the many manifestations of Coracle. Some constant qualities that spring to mind are suggested by the prevalence of the timeless raw materials of landscape, Englishness, gardens, water, interiors, weather, walking… tempered by a gut instinct to turn any first notion on its head, to pull the rug from under one's own feet rather than settle for the tired, the safe or the unexceptional. Whatever it adds up to includes at the very least an unerring eye for things of quality and freshness; and the expertise to place them beyond dispute.

Once their places
were set before

they entered, and
after, the rain

would not melt
their traces;

their shapes stay on
grass, and the shade

the wind blew
over their faces

is here again.

In 1964, Simon Cutts travelled from Belper, Derbyshire via bits of the rest of England and Europe, to West Bridgford, Nottingham, as an habitué of Stuart Mills's and Martin Parnell's Trent Bookshop. A common interest in poetry was established, and a common outlet in the expediency of small press publishing. Tarasque, "an animal which lived on the banks of the Rhone in France and ravaged the surrounding countryside until it was overcome," was already marked off in Mills's notebook for the name of a periodical. *Tarasque* was predatory enough in its vigorous criticism, found material and sideswipes at the literary establishment, but was simultaneously a showcase poetry magazine that published among others Spike Hawkins, Hugh Creighton Hill, Ronald Duncan and Ian Hamilton Finlay, and was principal platform for the poetry of Mills and Cutts.

Some of the spirit that contributes to any notion of *Coracle*, as also to the activities of Coracle, comes directly from the constant values in Simon Cutts's work as a poet. His poetry from this time entwined strands of the lyrical and pastoral with a musical sensibility and bluff language in works of sustaining lure and wit. Their stance, the *Coracle* stance, is evidently antithetical to the soul-searching confessional poem. As for what they were about, Stuart Mills in *Tarasque* 6 proposed: "The proper subjects for poetry are: the Seasons, the Affections, Fishing Boats, Inland Waterways, Non-Alcoholic Beverages, Certain Flowers, Certain Trees. Improper subjects are: Sex, Drugs, War and Self."

le Marché

I looked for
a lettuce
but bought
a petticoat

Tellingly, the influences on the written work were beyond the stock of the small press clique. French poetry of the 19th century; but also the Post Impressionists, Imagism, Vorticism, Joyce, Debussy… these were milestones at the cusp of symbolism and imagery. More immediate was

Lines on the Hoped-for Rejection from the Burnham Market Craft Fair

our thanks to Mr Archie Forrest
and his Committee, that
our work was not considered
Craft.

we continue to paddle
our Coracle in Docking
as if it were
a Raft.

1993

an admiration for the minstrelsy of contemporary lyrical poets such as Basil Bunting, Roy Fisher and Gael Turnbull. And through that filter, an awareness of such figures on the emerging concrete poetry scene as Robert Lax, Eugen Gomringer and Ian Hamilton Finlay.

Simon Cutts later suggested that concrete poetry had passed him by in the '60s, perhaps because he had by this time identified the metaphor, more than the word or the letter, as the unit of poetic transaction. Concrete poetry, to him, would be less an aesthetic bath than a new focus on elements of the poem that had traditionally been taken for granted. In 1975 he wrote:

> Whilst it now seems to me impossible to write even a 'lyrical' poem without some recourse to type structure and presence of 'line' bestowed by it, one begins to see other possibilities… [4]

One aspect of concrete that accorded with Cutts's own sensibilities, and was to be a constant in *Coracle*, was the promotion of brevity. *The artist has no right to waste the time of his audience* is a quote from Erik Satie that he thought central enough to reproduce in the limited edition of a rubber stamp carousel. It ties in to Ezra Pound's Imagist aesthetic of the poem as an intellectual and emotional instant; Pound, again, published what Basil Bunting had discovered, the translation of 'to poeticise' as 'to condense.'

The dread of the overwrought and unrestrained found its expression, characteristically, in *Tarasque* 10: "In TLS reviews of concrete poetry, for 'complex' read 'a horrible mess'."

> As for the verse, what sort
> of reality does it bear
> in sunlight, after the winter
> of close hills above the river
> and the tight view of pages
> under tungsten lighting
> Is it the same name
> it belongs to?

Simon Cutts remained open to the possibility of the magazine as testing ground, and more significantly as a polemical platform. This, with a fascination for the idea of the uniform series, would result ultimately in the non-magazine *Little Critic*, an open-ended uniform numbered pamphlet series founded in 1989. It might also be said that the magazine format would be converted to the needs of a gallery and bookshop, a *petit magasin*, at Coracle, where there would be much potential for delving and discovery.

But after the first few numbers of *Tarasque*, Cutts began to doubt the suitability of the magazine format for "everything we wanted to do."[5] Persuaded that "sometimes you need the entire context of the closed covers on a given single work," he and Mills published editioned work from 1965. The first few issues of *Tarasque* had been run off on the bog-standard mimeograph, which was used again for one or two editions, such as Spike Hawkins's *Poems* (1965). But running a small press meant being typographer, designer, printer, binder and publisher. For some, this was the last obligation of writing; elsewhere, as at Tarasque, the new regard for paper, type and assembly led to a promotion of the primacy of the publication. An example is Stuart Mills's *The Bridlepath is Filled with Clouds* (1969), in which text, a cut-out window and a halftone print of reflections in surface water make what might be booklet, print or fold-away sculpture.

That publication was farmed out to commercial offset printers; other editions were screenprinted, including Ian Hamilton Finlay's seminal typographic prints *Acrobats, Star/Steer* and *Sea Poppy* (all 1968). But if this work was to test the limits of printing, it would reach the limit of what commercial printers could be persuaded to do first. Hence the acquisition of a heavy-duty treadle platen letterpress machine, duly installed in a shed. It was powerful enough to print the blind impression on Simon Cutts's *A Doll's Ironing Board* (1972), and the relatively large text areas of *The Blue Boat Train* (1969). It could punch holes, as in

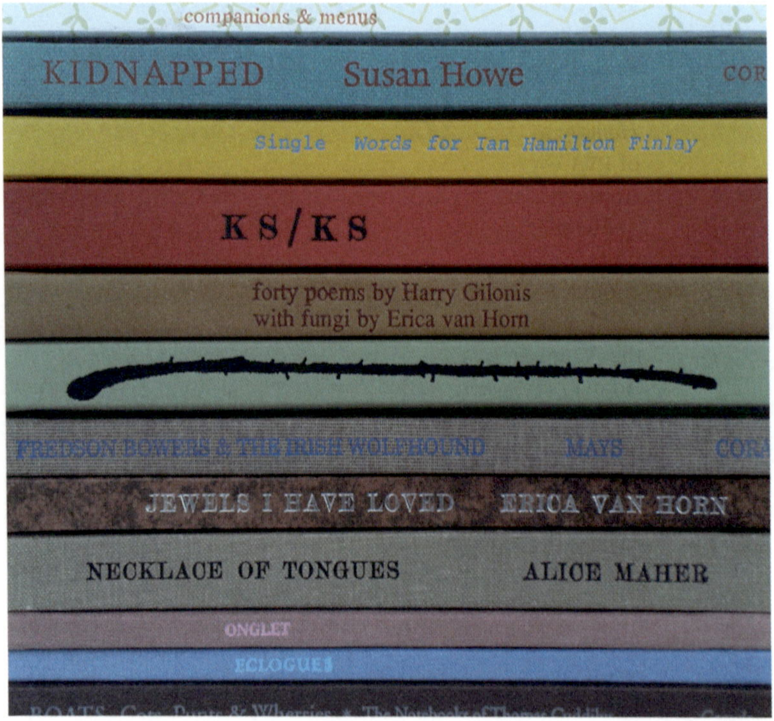
companions & menus
KIDNAPPED
Susan Howe
Single Words for Ian Hamilton Finlay
KS/KS
forty poems by Harry Gilonis
with fungi by Erica van Horn
FREDSON BOWERS & THE IRISH WOLFHOUND
MAYS
JEWELS I HAVE LOVED
ERICA VAN HORN
NECKLACE OF TONGUES
ALICE MAHER
ONGLET
ECLOGUES

the Martin Fidler and Simon Cutts Christmas card *Lucky Dip* (1973). Letterpress printing began to suggest its own possibilities, such as the three-colour text of *Thousands of Little Pieces of Cloth* (1970), an exercise in registration. It was even possible to go entirely off-piste, as with the iconic *Homage to G. Seurat* (1972), a card pasted with a rectangle of PVA over which hundreds and thousands were sprinkled (to the later bemusement of conservationists).[6]

The platen, together with the Adana tabletop printing press, a stripped-down, no frills letterpress machine light enough to carry in one hand, fitted Tarasque operations, and remained a cohesive force for the collective model: the Adana was a social machine, and the society of the Adana paired off countless permutations of two-person teams working as operator and feed. The one to load stock onto the platen, and work the impression lever; the other to remove, check and spread the printed sheet in a drying matrix. Good results were the reward of a fast and steady pace: a small print area on plain card might achieve a print run of 300 inside twenty minutes. Co-ordination had to be meticulous, for obvious reasons.

The clunk of the lead biting on paper and the ping of the revolving ink disc were the metronome of the small edition. The ultimate sanction, and homage, would have been Simon Cutts's proposed (but never realised) performance sculpture: an Adana chamber ensemble.

Flower

a word we have used

the e is petalled
by memory

Meanwhile, going into the 1970s, Cutts studied at Nottingham School of Art, where the foundations for the collectivist activities of the mid-'70s to '80s were laid, within practices shared with, among others, Ian Gardner, Stephen Duncalf, Martin Fidler, Martin Rogers and Kay Roberts, all of whom went on to run galleries or small presses. Another would-be Coracle aficionado, Stephen Skidmore, entered for his degree show a working greasy-spoon cafe constructed within the studios, exemplifying something of the emergent iconoclastic Nottingham ethic.

What would be the end point of Tarasque was signalled by an exhibition at the Midland Group Gallery, Nottingham, in 1972. *Metaphor and Motif* was the definitive title for the culmination of what Stuart Mills described as "something surprisingly consistent"[7] that had "been going on in Nottingham for the past few years": the engagement of the minimal poetry of Cutts and Mills with the effortless graphic art of Ian Gardner, the visual poetry of Ian

Hamilton Finlay, and the polemic of concrete poetry guru Stephen Bann in a complex of cross-references.

In the reassessment of the participants' positions at the outcome of the show, Cutts and Gardner embarked on a new joint venture with Karl Torok and Martin Fidler, *Blue Tunnel*, which was short-lived for "geographical, economic and even aesthetic reasons."[8] Blue Tunnel became the exclusive concern of Ian and Anne Gardner; Stuart Mills, remaining evangelical about the idea of the magazine, followed *Tarasque* with the immaculate *Aggie Weston's*; while Simon Cutts removed first to Moseley, Birmingham, to teach foundation and publish under his own name, and finally to London, where he rubbed shoulders with Richard Wilson and Anish Kapoor at Hornsey College of Art, and began publishing under the imprint Coracle Press.

late starlings

startled
by traffic

resettle

In the introduction to a second exhibition and catalogue for the Midland Group Gallery in the summer of 1975, *The Weather House and other works*, Simon Cutts wrote of

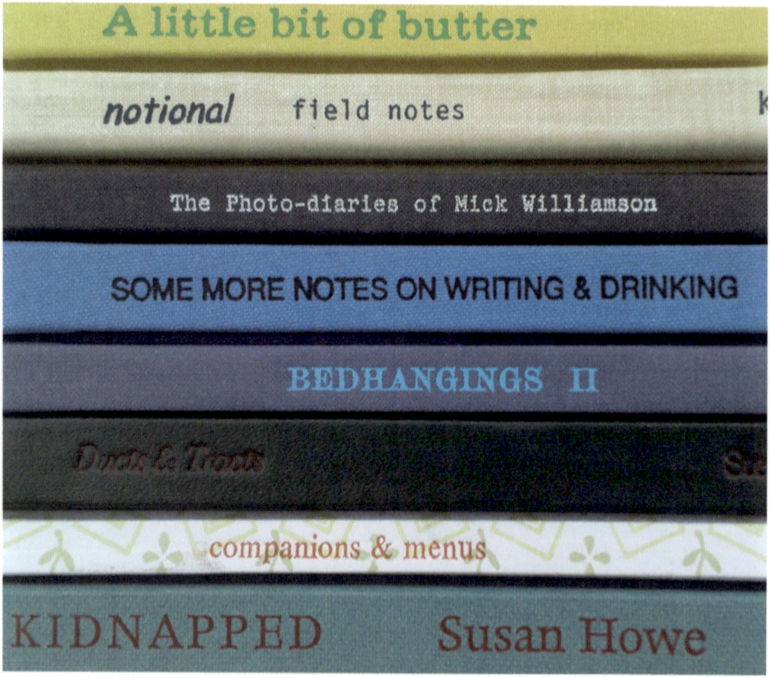
A little bit of butter
notional
field notes
The Photo-diaries of Mick Williamson
SOME MORE NOTES ON WRITING & DRINKING
BEDHANGINGS II
companions & menus
KIDNAPPED
Susan Howe

"an even further disintegration"[9] of the position of a small press complex since *Metaphor and Motif*, identifying the 'one-man operation' of Coracle with Ian Hamilton Finlay's Wild Hawthorn Press. Finlay was by this time a crucial figure, breaking conventions and broadening the scope of concrete poetry from its origins in experimental typography to embrace print, book and card formats, sculpture, photography, found art and poetry, and, within his garden at Stonypath, poetic objects and landscape interventions.

But whereas Finlay's own position was sustained through exemplary collaborative practices, Coracle was shucking off formal partnerships to craft a new, loose, organic collective. Writing of his singular position as "relegation," which was subject to re-appraisal "towards an unspoken objective," Cutts proposed:

> I still work with the notion to hand that the group phenomenon is the most important characteristic of the modern movement, in its pursuit of aesthetic centre. It still remains the only valid approach to a working position independent of the barriers that separate 'the arts'.[10]

The group, as manifest here, was centred around Nottingham contemporaries (many of whom, incidentally, would form an unofficial pool of collaborators working with Ian Hamilton Finlay in the 1970s, including not only both Cutts and Mills but also Martin Fidler, Karl Torok,

Stephen Duncalf and Ian Gardner). Painters, sculptors and poets, they were the foundation of a collective working, printing and exhibiting within and around Coracle, lending a potency and impetus beyond its own means.

The Weather House and other works was perhaps as close as anything to a demonstrative manifesto of Coracle, some of whose key signatures were identified in the catalogue as a preference for "a certain delicacy and slightness of key"; a pre-occupation with landscape; and "an element of obvious decorativeness." Here were, indeed, drawings of gardens, allotments and weather; the painting of a stylised train; aircraft camouflaged against cloud wall-paper in *A View Over the Skirting Board*; graphic elements from painting reassembled in a constructivist *Wadsworth Scrambler*; found images, poetry, criticism and artists' notes scattered without priority. It is hard to place a finger on exactly where lies its deceptive coherence.

Affections
confections

cakes
confetti

Shortly after, the 'unspoken objective' was found: a milliner's shop in a Georgian terrace in south London, perfectly suited for a gallery. Simon Cutts, in partnership with Kay Roberts, and with the small press and gallery expertise of new neighbour Brian Lane, undertook renovation, and Coracle Press opened its doors at 233 Camberwell New Road in July 1976.

One attribute was the doll's house-like proportions. Another was the integration, or rather reintegration of the living and working, visual and written, decorative and functional. Thus the hub of operations was, unusually for a gallery, a bookshop. Long after the demise of the Trent Bookshop, the idea of a bookshop being 'anchor,' the fulcrum for a working practice, remained a recurrent notion to Simon Cutts. It allowed the playing out of a very direct conceptual exchange: gallery walls as pages, and the book as a pocket exhibition.

An example of this that broke entirely new ground was Richard Wilson's *Wind Instruments* (1980), a flatpack edition in a wooden case of the wall-mounted sculptures that formed the first show in the Camberwell gallery. It was, in effect, an entire exhibition made portable, a totem of the equivalence of room and book. The sun-brandings of Roger Ackling's *Drawings from the Outer Hebrides* show were made available in silkscreen by Martin Rogers in two *Helping Hand* (1980) editions: one, tipped into a book, blotting paper bone folders boxes broadsheets button badges carrier bags case bindings catalogues cigarette cards coat hangers condiments covered sewn sections drawn on covers dry cleaners polythene covers dusters envelopes eye baths egg cups eye shades feather dusters fly posters grey board glass paperweights invitations leaflets library cards lollipop sticks luggage labels magazines manuscript paper mini printers mud prints neon newsletters paddles paper bags perfect bound blocks photocopies plaster boomerangs poetry postcards price lists rainhats readers tickets rice bowls rubber stamp carousels self adhesive labels sewn pamphlets shovels spectacles sugar tins tissue paper trellises viewmasters vitreous enamels whisks wine labels. **Coracle books at the King's Lynn Arts Centre 27-29 King Street King's Lynn Norfolk PE30 1HA Telephone 0553 774725 Facsimile 0553 770591 March 26th - May 14th 1994** the other a print. In the tradition of the *belle livre* was a portfolio of breathtakingly delicate prints of Len McComb's watercolour show, *Blossoms and Flowers* (1979). And on the occasion of his *Watermarks* exhibition at Coracle, Richard Long made the ultimate comment on the whole handmade, hand-printed fetish in *Mud Hand Prints* (1984), a case-binding of his left and right handprints in spattered Avon mud.

Coracle was one of a handful of independent non-commercial galleries in England in the 1970s and 80s. Non-commercial in that the artists were not on contract; art was not warehoused; exhibitions were not always 'selling' shows; and funds for individual projects arrived in the form of grants, loans, sponsorship and commissions. Each work, each show, made its own merit. One advantage was that Coracle could make its programme a star-gazey pie, with a view to broader horizons than the commercial gallery obligated to its own stable of artists. Another: a core of the audience of artists, curators and collectors became regulars, finding this a project worth supporting, its affability and lack of pretension a welcome alternative to the 'Art-U-Like' gallery shops of the West End.

Another Thumbprint:
Hedges and Hillsides

—more
of a landslide
with ditches.

"Are football
pitches
Landscape?"

I heard
the young
director
say

The gallery space was seen as an active element of the work, just as the programme of exhibitions would be seen as an artistic work in its own right. This would be celebrated in, for example, a series of poetry readings 'from the pulpit' (the boxed-in steps leading from front gallery to rear), and *Tongue & Groove*, an exhibition which borrowed its name from the wall cladding. Installations played up the quirks of the gallery, from Martin Rogers's mallet soundbox in place of a doorbell, to Anish Kapoor's annihilation of the gallery's uniform whiteness with red pigment. One of the final acts at 233 Camberwell New Road, Andy Goldsworthy's cutting a hole through the gallery lino into the *Evidence* of the sub-basement in 1985, brought the conceit full circle when the jagged disc of removed flooring became a linocut for the complementary publication.

Perhaps the apotheosis of this trope would occur in the chance discovery in 1984 of Edward Hopper's 1948 study of a New York shopfront, *7 A.M.* The painting's near-replication of the Camberwell gallery was startling enough as coincidence, more so as symbol of Coracle's credo of room and space as significant media. Stephen Duncalf was commissioned to convert the elements of the Coracle gallery that did not conform to the painting: a screen built behind the window counter, decorated with painted bottles and indecipherable advertising placards; a tin clock mounted on the wall, which was painted with morning shadows; a step built into the alcove of the front door, signed bottom right 'Edward Hopper'. Whether any of the passengers of the No. 36 buses stopping across the road ever noticed the gallery's reincarnation as a masterpiece of poignant realism, we don't know.

But it was the idiosyncratic group shows that did more than anything to bring in the crowds and introduce the notion of *Coracle*. The first, *Miniatures* (1977), a manifesto of the gallery's championship of the understated and unimposing, simultaneously made a wry disclaimer of the gallery's own 'miniature' status by cramming the walls and

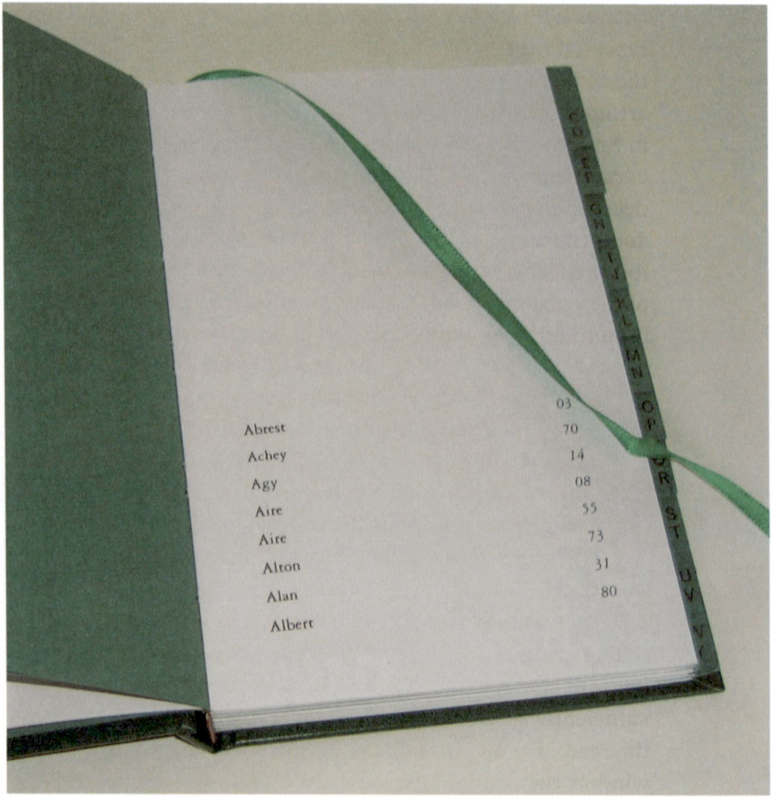
Abrest 03
Achey 70
Agy 14
Aire 08
Aire 55
Alton 73
Alan 31
Albert 80

shelves with the work of 100 artists. *Fo(u)ndlings* (1978) repeated the trick in a show that took found art out of the academic corral, while *On Loan* showcased borrowed art in the winter of 1980. The potency of the group show, in Simon Cutts's hands an act of the most polemical curatorship, was demonstrated again in *Artists Blocks*, a deceptive *open sesame* to the hermetic practices of print and printmaking. These, and other group shows that have followed, showed an unexpected side to the work of many of the participants, and offered something of a testing ground for new work, just as *Tarasque* had for new writing.

ash falls as
asterisks

spaciousness, snow

⋆

The printing effort that had begun in garden sheds and beneath staircases continued in the Coracle basement, sufficiently sunken to give a dog's-eye view of the garden to the rear, and back into the front gallery through a monk's window beneath the pulpit. It made a compact print room, with much of the space taken by two massive items from an Edwardian jobbing printshop, in the form of treadle platen and cast iron guillotine. A typecase was wedged into the hearth, Victorian sink in the alcove, and an Adana atop a kitchen table. Printing here was entirely tangible and physical, the bringing together of metal, ink, paper, board, thread and paste, and sometimes less conventional materials.

The printing and publishing programme now interspersed 'press' books, booklets and cards with gallery ephemera, including invitation cards,[11] announcements, booklists and catalogues, in a continual spectrum that quite deliberately challenged categorization: some of the ephemera[12] is as highly considered—and collectible—as the top-end limited editions. Technically, demands from the gallery programme and extensions to available printing resources fed off each other. The rubber stamp, referenced from time to time, became celebrated in *The Rubber Stamp Mini-printer Series* in 1993; thermography, glazing powder sprinkled on fresh ink and wafted across a one-bar electric fire, jazzed up the Christmas card for 1977; collotype was the only medium for an invitation card for Stephen Skidmore's pencil drawings; hand-colouring used sparingly, of for example the sycamore samara on the cover of *The Coracle in Docking*; while that Benny Hill of reprographics, the great potato cut, was used to smack a livid green Coracle logo onto the 1982 list of forthcoming exhibitions: an apparently arbitrary ticking off of one more printing technique, until one remembers the resemblance of a coracle for a bisected potato.

of mundanity
and defunct
material

an alchemy:

the glue-gun's
transparent
secretions

of silver
thread.

beyond design

the rightness
and finesse
of roughness
of purpose

The elephant in the Coracle bookroom is design. There is, in Coracle's back catalogue, a sense of a conscious effort to subvert the notion of design, to skip that phase in

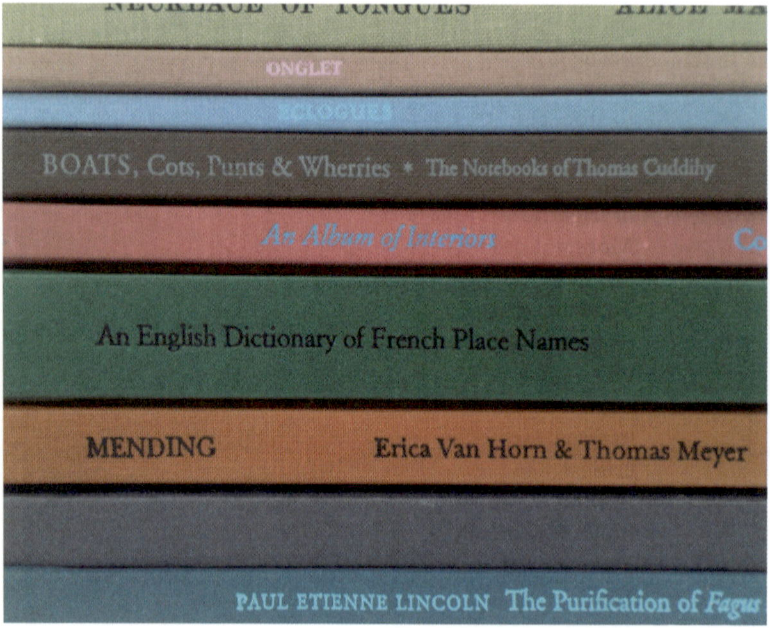
ONGLET
BOATS, Cots, Punts & Wherries * The Notebooks of Thomas Cuddihy
An Album of Interiors
An English Dictionary of French Place Names
MENDING
Erica Van Horn & Thomas Meyer
PAUL ETIENNE LINCOLN
The Purification of Fagus

publication when heads are put together to convert ideas into visual or conceptual 'statements' (a phase elsewhere increasingly to the fore). Briefly: integral good, imposed bad. So the 'design' of Coracle publications has most often been surrogate, something that emerges from the play of content against material. The virtue lies in knowing when to stop, and quite often stopping sooner.

The process here is central to *Coracle,* a stepping-stone path guided by notions of what is 'true,' or 'honest,' or 'right.' None of these is, in this context, absolute. More, this depends on an instinctive adherence not to any design dogma, but to an unspoken poetic rationale. To take one example: in 1983 Simon Cutts chanced in conversation upon the German construct *Schaufelbagger und Muldenkipper* (excavator and tipper truck). As a self-contained linguistic moment it seemed too good to waste; its 'true' application came as headline for a show taking a critical stance on the clunky British sculpture of the time. For the catalogue cover, ink applied to the tracks of a toy bulldozer turned it into a printing machine. The blocks and gaps of the printed track suggested a section of spiral binding, which so became 'right' for the spine. Vinyl boards and an exaggerated landscape format made this a manual for hard-hat areas. And for the invitation card, a child's plastic spade was perfect to subvert the machismo of the roadworking machinery, but was felt too gestural alone.

The square was circled with a sandpaper cut-out glued to the blade; the exhibition details became a manufacturer's tag tied to the handle. Voila.

Elsewhere, meretricious design has been avoided by the use of idiom. This has sometimes been almost literal, as for example a catalogue for the Camden Arts Centre's *1984* exhibition. The title carried such a weight of inference that it seemed a design cliché was unavoidable, and so the question was put: what do you think of when you think of 1984? The answer round the table was, of course, Orwell's novel, in an old Penguin edition. So a new old Penguin was hammered out in ration-era white, black and orange, letterpress on pulp, all the remaining elements of design a simple paint-by-numbers exercise.

A danger of idiomatic design is that slight exaggeration or over-emphasis can be enough to turn the exercise into parody, the accent now a transparent mockney, the purpose seemingly a craving for street-cred. An example of how it may be done well was the small catalogue of a Russian neo-constructivist, *Oleg Kudryashov* (1984), in which colour printing on the 'wrong' absorbent paper was all that was needed to precipitate thoughts of melancholia, Malevich and soviet utilitarianism. At other times the idiom was extended or transformed. For the *Miniatures* show, the catalogue was condensed down to a small packet the size of a box of sweet cigarettes, and filled with cards, one for each artist, redolent of a collection of football cards. The *On Loan* catalogue followed its own inevitability in being a file box of library tickets, while *Fo(u)ndlings* was printed on a swatch of luggage labels. A late contender, *The South Bank Show*, a pan-South London showcase, continued the boxed-card theme with what might have been media cue-cards.

The physicality of these catalogues brings them close to another *Coracle* landmark: found and editioned objects. These have been sufficiently remarked upon to have provoked listing, from blotting paper to wine labels, on an invitation card, *Coracle Books at the King's Lynn Arts Centre*, 1994. Some, such as rain hats (for the critic who complained that he didn't go to South London because it was always raining), coat hangers (for Michael Petry's *Auto-Didactic* painted clothes), dusters (for the V&A Museum vitrines) and trellises (for Martin Rogers's outdoor sculpture), were sent out as invitations. Editioned objects, the sculptural equivalent of print, include paper weights (*Maidenhair*, Simon Cutts 1975) and Bill Culbert's sugar tin light-box. Some were without occasion, such as bone-folders and a job lot of editor's eyeshades, printed with the Coracle logo and given away as loyalty cards; others as ephemeral as Yoko Terauchi's wax-paper origami rice bowls in which lunch was served one May Day.

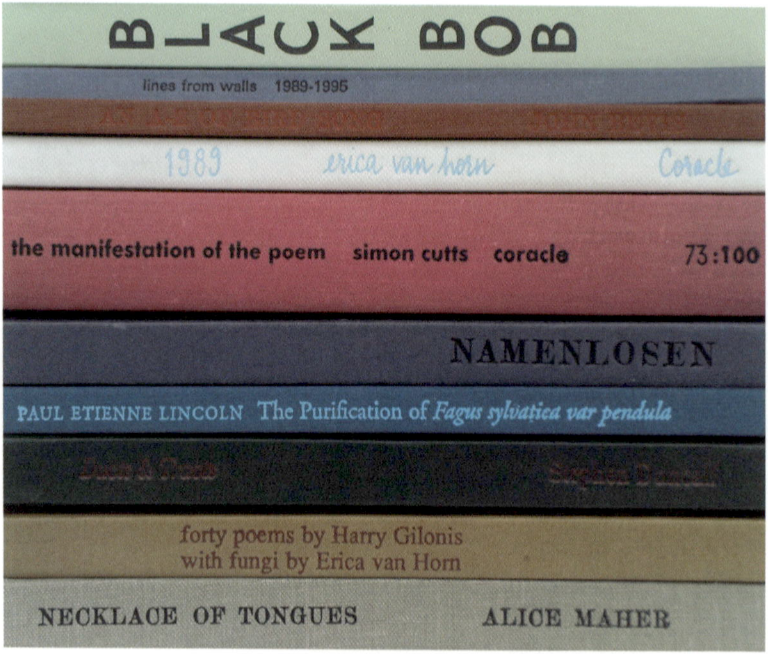
BLACK BOB
lines from walls 1989-1995
1989 erica van horn Coracle
the manifestation of the poem simon cutts coracle 73:100
NAMENLOSEN
PAUL ETIENNE LINCOLN The Purification of Fagus sylvatica var pendula
forty poems by Harry Gilonis
with fungi by Erica van Horn
NECKLACE OF TONGUES ALICE MAHER

a goldfish
bowl

filled with
golf balls

The flip side to DIY, as the Tarasque experience acknowledged, is the use of commercial printers and print finishers working to specification. At entry level this is simply using a copy shop for reprographics, and many examples on the Coracle list of publications are executed in this way. At least one, *Video Times*, produced to accompany Kevin Atherton's installation at the Ikon Gallery in 1984, was run off on the Coracle photocopier in imitation of cheap high street dry printing.

Some of the Coracle output called for more recondite means. This was, on the one hand, making a deal with availability; on the other, a fascination with outposts of the printing trade discovered, via perambulations through London's byways, chasing their destiny to some Dickensian conclusion. Johel were the Morris-dancing typesetters working through a fug of spraymount in Kennington Lane; paper merchants T. N. Lawrence, in the sun-bleached glory of their warehouse in Bleeding Heart Yard, provoked the paper-swatch tribute *English Coloured*

Papers;[13] the trade counter of Adana's letterpress supplies in Gray's Inn Road could have inspired the set from Ronnie Barker's 'four candles' sketch; while at Bowling Green Lane, Harry Palmer in his biro-skidded warehouse coat ran a grotto producing printing blocks for Fleet Street, and solved the then-thorny problem of how to reproduce the camera-invisible blue ink of Susan Hiller's automatic writing for *Sisters of Menon* (1983).

At the top end was a two-way pay-off, in which the printer brought something to Coracle that might not otherwise have been possible or conceived of. This was in part a meeting of kindred spirits, in part professional curiosity about testing the boundaries of normal print practice. Terry Cook at Edward Wells & Sons, a hundred yards up the Camberwell New Road, was such a case. The premises itself fitted curiously the Coracle format, the house-above-the-shop façade giving no hint of the Heidelberg and linotype machinery within. Here one might lose half a day, or even a day if feet could withstand the ice-cold concrete of the machine room floor, pulling proofs, adjusting inking, pressure and registration, trying out different papers, editing on the hoof, working towards some ordained outcome, gathering evidence towards future printing possibilities.

Very often the means of production were mixed and layered one on the other. A concertina booklet to accompany Bernard Lassus's show *Les Pins* (1983) for example, included commercial four-colour offset printing squeezed onto the margins of another job; a text section phototypeset and printed in a copyshop; the cover printed letterpress and creased on an Adana; trimming by guillotine; folding, stitching and gluing all done by hand. A showcase of this way of working was the *Tongue and Groove* (1983) catalogue, whose cover alone featured cut-outs, paper inserts, offset, blind printing, hand colouring, tied thread and eye rivets.

> An opportunity of the intimate gallery which we cherish… is to place well and enjoy little masterpieces for small furnished rooms.[14]

By 1982, the gallery had expanded; literally, since Kay Roberts had acquired the next-door premises, number 235, and the gallery rooms now occupied the ground floors of both buildings. There was a collective[15] employed full-time on a programme of printing, exhibitions and admin; an expanding backlist of publications; a queue of exhibition proposals; a regular clientele of artists, collectors, critics and enthusiasts. Simon Cutts, in partnership with Margot Hapgood, found themselves in a dialect between city and landscape, urban time and rural space. Weekend motoring trips eventually settled on a house in Docking, Norfolk, which they renovated for a new project. This would be

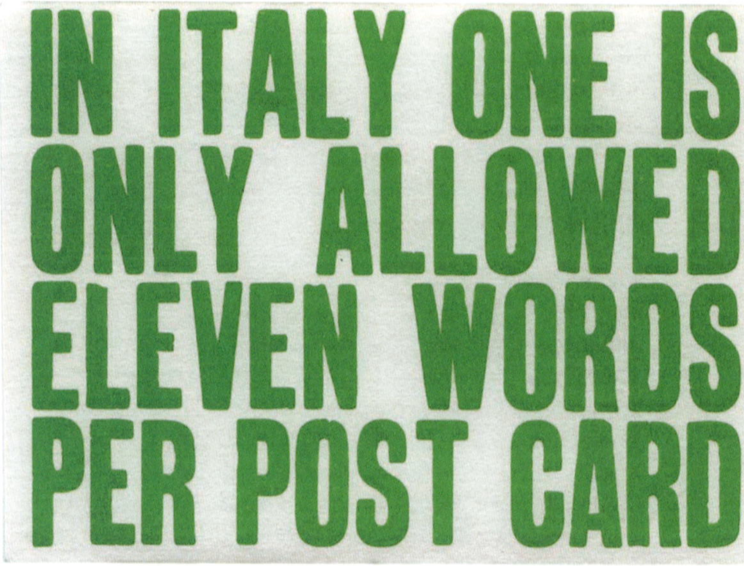
IN ITALY ONE IS
ONLY ALLOWED
ELEVEN WORDS
PER POST CARD

home to their permanent collection as well as a gallery space, where artists could work in residency towards an exhibition and publication. The whole would be a model of art in domesticity, in the manner of Jim Ede's Kettle's Yard, with nods to Ian Hamilton Finlay's Stonypath garden and the hindsight of Shaker living. Tragically, Margot Hapgood was to die in 1985; for now, plans to expand Coracle in Norfolk were put on hold.

The Norfolk experience restored to London a new urgency, a restlessness. There was a sense of loyalties being torn between the idealised unit of gallery, bookshop and press under one roof, and the infinite possibilities that might arise from exposing the ethics and work practices that supported Coracle projects to altogether new situations. Thoughts turned to galleries in the West End, New York, Europe; barnstorming non-gallery spaces for temporary exhibitions; bookshop franchises; an artists' books agency. The next few years would see Coracle engage in a gamut of possibilities.

Already there was a programme of making books on commission, working with artists whose niche was securely carved elsewhere, in formats beyond the normal bread and butter of Coracle. This had begun in 1980 with the photo concertina *A Walk Past Standing Stones*, the first of four Richard Long publications for Anthony d'Offay, and would continue with further long-term working relationships and exemplary books for Hamish Fulton, David Tremlett, Susan Hiller, Stephen Willats and Antony Gormley, among others.

Now, invitations were arriving for Coracle to assemble outreach exhibitions as a commando operation for foreign spaces. There was a cerebral exercise in assembling a group show, principally of sculpture, for installation in new spaces, such as the Puck Building in New York (*Assemble Here!*) or Rees Martin's art warehouse in South London (*Low Tech*) that made an equation of artist, work, and working relationship; who could be called on for what end; how space and work might play off each other; what would be the fruits of provocation. *Plux Value* (1984) was a punkish exchange show with the Eric Fabre Gallery in Paris, while in 1986 *The Unpainted Landscape* shared a critical attitude to home-grown land art with a large audience, via a tour of Scottish galleries.

Coracle had selected an exhibition of artists' books for the Frankfurter Kunstverein in 1981, and curated a further show of its own books in 1983 for Riverside Studios, *Under One Roof*. The idea of an outreach bookshop was tested at the hub of Coracle's share of a show of three artists' galleries at the Serpentine Gallery in 1984, *Salon d'Automne;* how intractably this pitted Coracle sensibilities against those of the Arts Council was epitomised in Bill Culbert's work for the show of strip lights piercing the veranda doors, which had to be recreated in replica within the confines of the gallery rooms for health and safety reasons.

The possibility of a permanent bookshop embedded within a sympathetic space was mooted with the opening of the temporary exhibitions annexe at Kettle's Yard. Coracle bidded for the space with a prospectus that emphasized its pedigree in making artists' books, its international connections, its sympathy with the ethics of the museum/non-museum of Ede's house and permanent collection. The bookshop stock would provide a link between the inner and outer worlds of the gallery, just as it would with a spectrum of commercial and non-commercial publishing. In the first months of its opening Paul Lincoln had installed in its upstairs room his metaphorical bestiary *In Praise of Madame de Pompadour and the Court of Louis XV,* which was to run for the whole summer of 1985. And when Whitechapel Art Gallery opened its doors after Nicholas Serota's renovation, the Kettle's Yard bookshop was taken as a model and Coracle was asked to apply the same approach to running its own bookshop.

The culmination of Coracle's break-out was a new exhibition and education space at Renshaw Hall, Liverpool. The refurbishment of these huge premises was Coracle working on a grand scale, and with a grand title: Coracle Atlantic, "one of the very few serious attempts to de-centralise our activities, and to work in a new uncluttered and unprejudiced situation."[16] Liverpool: last port of call

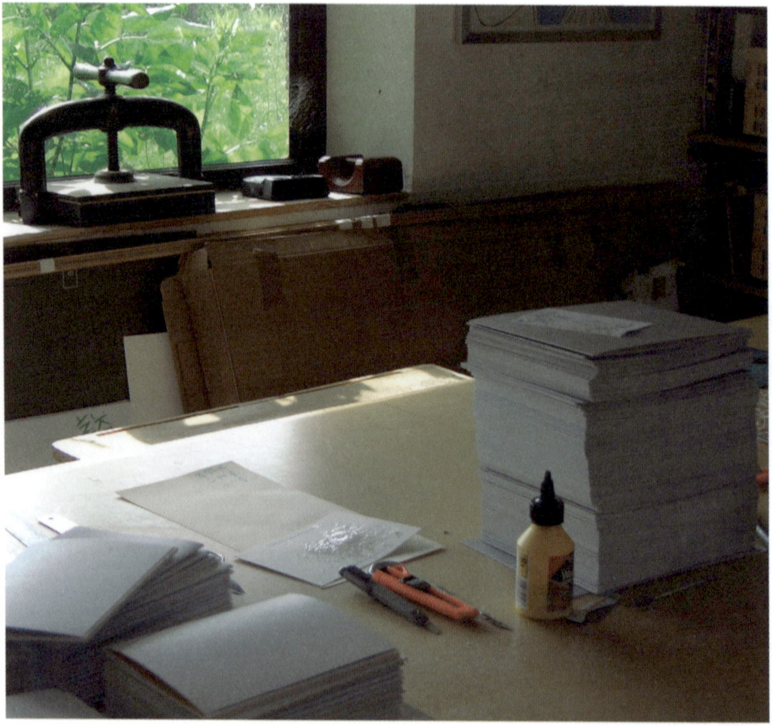

for the English exile. Renshaw Hall's history was archetypal Liverpudlian: dance hall, dole office and now arts complex. The cavernous space, a turbine hall of the north with potential for siting the single, gob-smacking grand oeuvre, was in 1987 perfectly realised in the first exhibition, a Richard Long stone rectangle *Stone Field*.

did Ian
Hamilton
Finlay
make

a Kettle's
Yard
Eccles
cake

?

Some of Coracle's corporate restlessness may have lodged in the stratosphere. In 1985 Victoria and Warren Miro had arrived at Camberwell (perhaps not their first port of call) with a proposal. They had secured the vacant Robert Fraser Gallery[17] space in Cork Street, and needed a partner with the contacts and know-how to establish a contemporary gallery. It was a timely proposal for the expansive mood at Coracle, and the deal that was struck included the wholesale gallery armoury of artists, programme, publications and management.

The politics of the Cork Street project caused some soul-searching. From Simon Cutts's point of view, Coracle was 'the project,' an organic entity in its own right, and the vehicle of his life-work. It was—gallery, bookshops, publications and all—an encompassing artwork, a Merzbau. Cork Street would be portal to an even greater inclusivity. But for some of those associated with the homely Camberwell project, Cork Street's connotations were antithetical: dressed in Armani, daunting and superficial, it seemed the showcase for a graftless and rootless art.

So it was a diplomatic triumph that saw the work of Stephen Duncalf, cabbage-patch vorticist, on the walls of Cork Street. There were star turns from the old gang, David Connearn, Richard Tuttle, Alan Charlton and Yoko Terauchi among them. The series of group exhibitions that Cutts had instigated 15 years earlier with *Metaphor and Motif*—shows that were edgy, timely and substantial beyond the sum of their parts—continued here with no less assurance in *Foto-Cliché*, *Entre La Mer et le Terre*, and *Furniture Sculpture*. But the dynamics of the commercial showroom were irrepressible, and jarred against contextual work: a show by Ian Hamilton Finlay, for instance, looked as never before perilously close to window dressing. Publications were in danger of being sidelined as publicity. Coracle's own gallery began for the first time to feel irrelevant. It felt as though Cork Street was leading Coracle into an impasse.

Then came the rather English gesture of starting afresh in Italy. Victoria Miro saw the potential for a contemporary gallery to expand the programme into Europe, and Simon Cutts and Erica Van Horn were to be ambassadors to Firenze. Coracle would continue here, in parallel but at a certain aesthetic distance from the showroom gallery: the freshness and rawness of the materials and work that were produced during this interlude are witness to a new inclusiveness determined through the work of Cutts and Van Horn working together and apart: focussing in on the immediate concerns of place and person, of living, working, eating, talking and learning, exemplified in Erica Van Horn's *Italian Lessons* series.

The Coracle diaspora was wrapped up in short order. In 1986, a show by herman de vries had been the swansong of the Camberwell gallery, by this time sited exclusively in 235 Camberwell New Road. Funds raised from the sale of the property were put up as collateral for Coracle Atlantic. But in Liverpool, reliance on sponsorship and central funding fell foul of the ousting of the old political order, and Renshaw Hall was closed. The franchise bookshops were the battleground for a debate between integrity and commercial viability, which eventually proved irreconcilable. The Coracle / Victoria Miro partnership was dissolved after

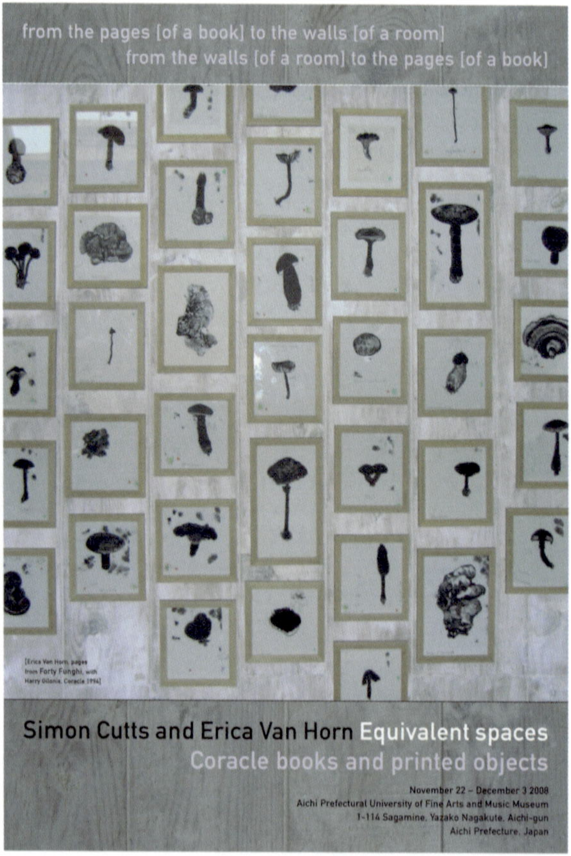
from the pages [of a book] to the walls [of a room]
from the walls [of a room] to the pages [of a book]
[Erica Van Horn, pages from Forty Funghi, with Harry Gilonis, Coracle 1994]
Simon Cutts and Erica Van Horn Equivalent spaces
Coracle books and printed objects
November 22 – December 3 2008
Aichi Prefectural University of Fine Arts and Music Museum
1-114 Sagamine, Yazako Nagakute, Aichi-gun
Aichi Prefecture, Japan

the Firenze project rejected a move to make it a player in an unrelated financial network.

The lifeline of Coracle to date was reprised in an exhibition and comprehensive catalogue for the Yale Center for British Art, in 1989–90: the cover image of *The Coracle* is a backs-to-the-wall panorama of the Camberwell roadscape.

Alter the syntax
of your name. Tamper
with the Capital letters.

Go unknown through
the French windows to
the draped sky.

1991. Simon Cutts and Erica Van Horn returned to Norfolk, to re-focus purely on publication. Aside from the cessation, for now, of publishing as adjunct to a visual programme, other influences and energies came to bear on the reconstituted Coracle: not least those of Erica Van Horn herself, an established New England book artist with whom Simon Cutts had begun a relationship in 1988. This evolved into marriage and a living and working partnership with shared responsibility for matters Coracle, a position that has informed operations for more than 20 years.

Erica Van Horn's work[18] is founded on distinct premises, such as Proustian associations with materials, as evidenced in her first Coracle publication, *Jewels I Have Loved* (1990), and again in *Two Peelings: 1993 & 2004*; formalised commemoration of the after-life of remnants, such as *Scraps of An Aborted Collaboration* (1994); a keen eye for etiquette, misunderstanding, faux pas and makeshift social adornments, suggested mischievously in the *Docking Competitions* of 1995, *Italian Lessons* and some of the subsequent *Living Locally* series of books and cards. The autobiographical element is central, and the work reveals the humours of a life of rugged competence liable to be trounced from the periphery, and the cares of the inadvertent custodian.[19] Her printmaking background is evident in hand-crafted and calligraphic work that captures the moment of engagement with the articulated immediacy of an acid splash on an etching. In a similar way her writing, as well sampled on her blog *The Journal—Living Locally*,[20] is pared back to acute and deadpan observation.

The influence of Erica Van Horn on Coracle output has been manifold. It opened up the possibility, for example, of aligning the self-publishing sector more closely with the artist-and-poet partnership of long-standing friends Tom and Laurie Clark in their own Cairn Gallery & Editions and Moschatel Press. In the event she and Simon Cutts have pursued their individual projects with a sparing number of books and cards appearing under joint names: *Sans Signaux* in 1990, and the substantial *Aglio 6 Olio* two years later; more recently and typical of the collaboration, two letterpress concertinas in 2008: a field guide to orchards in *8 Old Irish Apples*, and a delving into linguistic back-alleys in a vocabulary of local vernacular words for *Short-cuts*. More to the point, and as significant, has been Erica Van Horn's role in Coracle as measure and counterbalance, seeing the evolution of projects through discussion and shared decisions.

A rental unit in Docking, Norfolk, became Docking Warehouse, an entirely pragmatic, made for purpose workshop and storage facility for Coracle books. 'Availability' was the new watchword, the warehouse operation identified centrally within the dynamic of work, a gyroscope to maintain course through what Simon Cutts describes as "the ambivalence of intention, survival and commerce."[21] The Norfolk project took Coracle book production into new working relationships with Richard Crome of local printers Crome & Akers, and trade binder Stuart Settle. There were parallels here with the collaborative work with Wells & Sons in Camberwell, but with a new austerity. Whereas Wells adapted their jobbing-printing practice to meet bespoke demands halfway, the tendency of the Norfolk printers was to encapsulate commissions within their own house style. This was plain

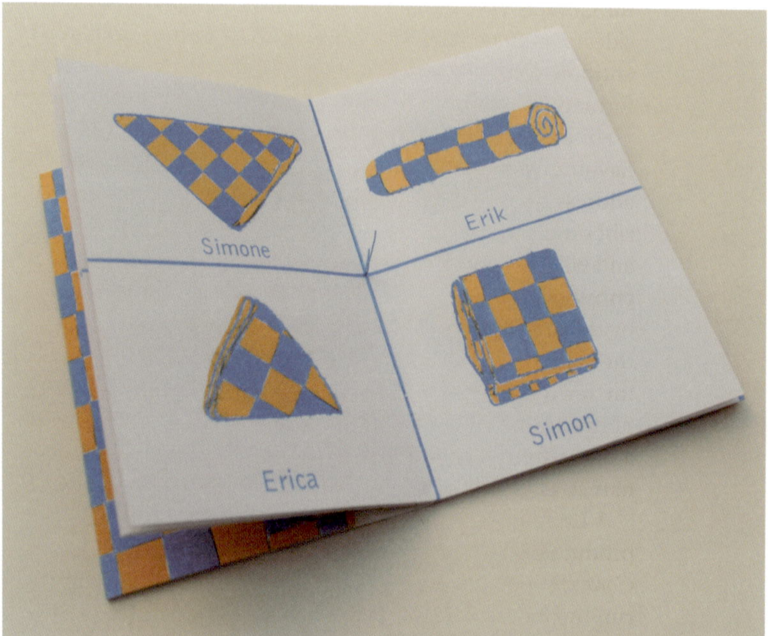
Simone
Erik
Erica
Simon

and meticulous, black and square, with a neutral regularity that recalls stationery more than book work. The attractions for Coracle were clear: the bugbear of design could be sidestepped, and the new coherence of production was antidote to haphazard titles produced to the benchmark format-follows-content aesthetic.

An English Dictionary of French Place Names gives a flavour: ostensibly not far removed from an off-the-shelf address book, complete with thumb-index dividers and ribbon placemark, the book is an alphabetical log of towns and villages visited in France whose names have an English currency: "Machine / Magenta / Magnet…", referenced by department code. The authentication that distinguishes the valid conceptual work from the desk-exercise comes in the form of photographs of road signs and reproductions of notes; and the final twist, a denouement in the shape of a quote from David Jones: "Pronounce all French place names as in English."

A London base and bookshop front for Norfolk production was established in 1993 as workfortheeyetodo, *Coracle* if not Coracle. In its first manifestation a bookshop run by photographer and book artist David Bellingham at Kay Roberts's New Exhibitions of Contemporary Art base in Narrow Street, it was rethought at new premises found in 1995 in Hanbury Street, Brick Lane. Here an adaptable bookshop / studio / workshop was set up, with reading, event and display space. The bookshop ran under the scrupulous invigilation of Maggie Smith, who matched knowledge of contemporary art publishing with a flair for display, and an invaluable sixth sense for connecting the browser with the thing they would most relish.

"We have never been so surrounded by career anarchists,"[22] lamented Simon Cutts, finding post-Thatcher London a melting-pot of "faddish conceptualism" promoted by a new creature, the 'curator-property speculator.' Workfortheeyetodo was isolated—or perhaps spared—by the lack of historical understanding of artist-run spaces. A perfect meeting of minds for the new stripped-down, urban art-activist Coracle came with Gustav Metzger, radical spirit of 1930's intellect, whose *Damaged Nature, Auto-destructive Art* (1996) book could have been a New Coracle Bible for metropolitan flare-out.

Anything may, with strict propriety
be called perfect
which perfectly answers
the purpose for which
it was made:

a packet of seeds

During a residency at the Irish Museum of Modern Art in 1996, Simon Cutts and Erica Van Horn walked round the bend in a boreen in Ballybeg and saw the potential of a property for the beginnings of the latest phase: a house and retreat in rural Ireland. Coracle here is a homestead, whose outhouses are studio, warehouse and print room; a farm for books. Visitors sleep in an artwork, a bedroom that is entirely an envelope installation by Erica Van Horn. One building has a grass roof; somewhere beyond the wild flower garden is a Museum of the Single Book.

This, of course, has taken years to achieve. Simon Cutts and Erica Van Horn's position in Ireland has demanded continual reassessment of the merits of determination and isolation, the more so with the closure of the London base at workfortheeyetodo in 1998. Coracle in Ireland is very much a two-person venture, while remaining informed by a Coracle ghost collective of artists, writers and book artists that functions now by email, post and phone. A key consultant is long-term collaborator on book projects, Colin Sackett, whose own output as a book artist[23] is a substantial library of investigations into time, place, order and pattern, by use of spatial typography, text and photography. His particular point of reference is the book—paper, print and binding—and his work *per se* book art, of publications that could only exist in their final form. This rigorous approach, combined with fastidious production ethics and

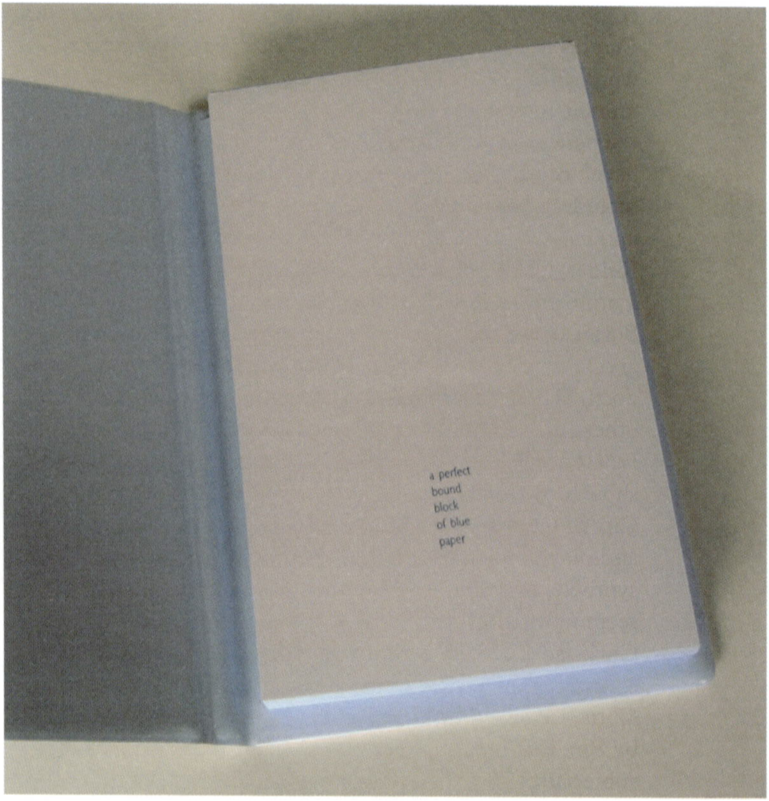
a perfect
bound
block
of blue
paper

comprehensive knowledge and understanding of things *Coracle*, makes him perhaps the one book designer able to work within Coracle practices and beneath the radar of graphic intrusion.[24]

There are, too, new connections made in Ireland who have become part of Coracle's publishing programme, including Maud Cotter (*also*, a letterpress concertina, and *other attachments*, four labels in a wallet); Cralan Kelder, whose poetry was published in *Lemon Red*, first of a uniform series with cover drawing by Erica Van Horn; Susan Howe, *Bedhangings II* (2002); and cartographer and land artist Tim Robinson (*The Vegetable Plot at L8511*, 2003). These artists and poets were selected, alongside others including Christian Bok, Maurizio Nannucci and Lawrence Weiner, by Simon Cutts as contributors to a show he originated and curated for the Cork: European City of Culture events of 2005. *Vinyl* was a jaunty and playful installation show that set responses to the synthetic materiality of the title against the context of the seemingly pre-plastic archaism of the environment of the Christian Brothers School at Sullivans Quay, Cork.

Another show proposed and curated from Ireland by Cutts, *Certain Trees*, borrowed its title from both a line by Roy Fisher and Stuart Mills's dictum on the proper subjects for poetry, quoted above. The exhibition celebrated the work of book artists in the Coracle orbit, including

Thomas A Clark and Laurie Clark, Les Coleman, Ian Hamilton Finlay and Robert Lax, with perhaps ten others who had worked closely within Coracle or Tarasque as well as running their own presses. It opened at the Centre des Livres d'Artistes at St Yrieix la Perche in 2006 before travelling to the Van Abbemuseum, Eindhoven, and V&A Museum, London, at each of those very different venues transcending the difficulties of a display of books under glass with contrasts of scale, colour and material, becoming so visually engaging that it took many visitors a while to realise this was a book show.

Certain Trees included an envelope constellation by Erica Van Horn, who showed another large-scale installation at Aichi University Museum, Japan, in 2008. Her collection of patterned and coloured envelope interiors has been a long-standing project. Their curiosity is that they are throwaways, unnoticed and often unseen, arbitrary designs without 'designerly' function whose purpose is expressly to conceal, while being themselves concealed. In this they become metaphors for something rather intimate, and there is a sense for the viewer of being let in somewhere secret, Alice Through the Envelope. As well as gallery projects and the Ballybeg guestroom, some have been editioned in xerox & letterpress pamphlets and casebound publications, from *Boy Bell's Book of Envelope Interiors* of 1993, which ran into three editions, through 1994's *Envelope Interiors*, the offset edition of *Airmail Envelope Interiors* in 2002, and *An Album of Interiors* (2008).

Simon Cutts, too, has concentrated in Ireland on larger-scale artworks, in his case a series of projects at the boundaries of text and sculpture: *Nine Poems*, a wall stencil work at Cairn Gallery, 1994; the *transhumance* neon for Jamie Warde-Aldam's library, 1999; further neon pieces for the ArtBarns project; the *anyone* bridge in Jamie Warde-Aldam's woodland, 2000. An earlier publication, *The History of the Airfields of Lincolnshire*, has been realised as an installation made from runway and cast aluminium letters.

His publications in this later period consolidate a number of concerns. The ornamental was noted as an area of interest in *The Weatherhouse*, and the ornamented book a preoccupation of Simon Cutts since, perhaps, the joint publication with Martin Fidler of *The Allies* (1974), with its scalpel-cut and folded-down cover stitched into place with an adhesive paper button. Working on the theme of the publication propelled by the possibilities of its own production has informed, for example, *Mirroirs*, with its reflective endpapers and mirror-printing; *Feuilles Albumesques,* which takes its cue from a reminiscence of the boards, guards and interleaved tissue of the traditional photograph album; and the latest in the range, the playful *onglet* of 2009, a unique testament of crazy logic.

Related to this is the contention of format as intelligible

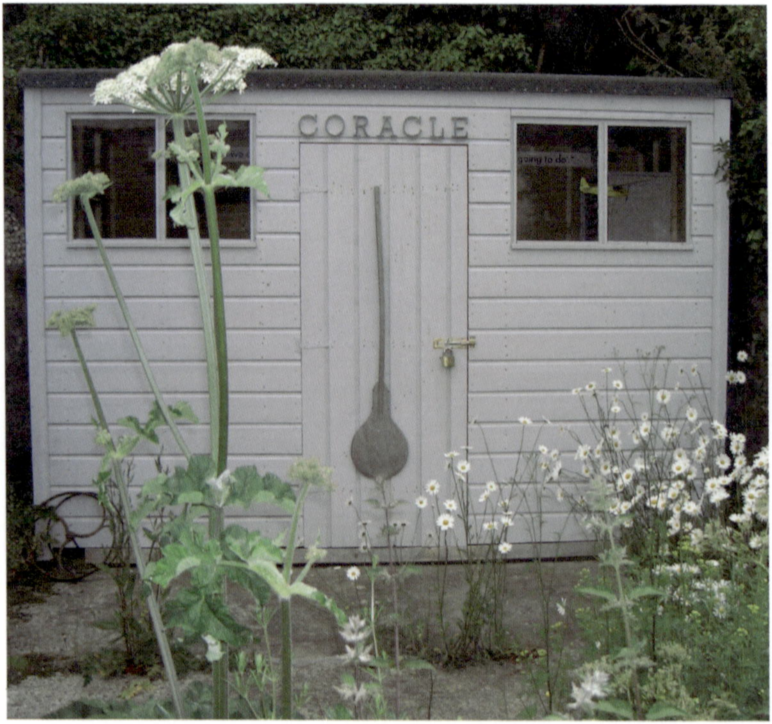
CORACLE

medium, explored in some of the early group show catalogues, *Miniatures* for example. *The Waterfalls of New Hampshire in Winter* (1994), a perfect-bound pad in a plastic wallet, creates in itself a visual metaphor, the economy of resources a riposte to the abundance of the waterfall in full flow, while in a small whirlpool of the mind the notions of stationery, the stationary nature of the paper pad, and the ceaseless motion of the water play out.

The possibility of working with other publishers has emerged as particularly advantageous in the cataloguing of Coracle and its allied work. Historically this has included Southampton Art Gallery (*4 Years at Coracle Press*) and Yale (*The Coracle*); current fruitful relationships exist in particular with Granary Books and Martin Rogers's RGAP (Research Group for Artists Publications). These collaborations have enabled a neutral platform for collected and annotated reference works, including an appreciation of the life and work of long-time Coracle collaborator Brian Lane edited by Simon Cutts, *The Printed Performance*; critical texts by Simon Cutts in *Some Forms of Availability*; and the work of Erica Van Horn in *The Book Remembers Everything*.

The notion of the professional small-press publisher is something of a paradox, but Cutts and Van Horn survive beyond the publishing programme through book commissions, installation commissions, teaching residencies and exhibition curatorships. Books continue to be printed and bound in Norfolk; smaller items in Ireland. Cards, postcards and ephemera prolong the Italian habit with work that takes a wry, if not scurrilous, look at the artists' place in their environment. Among these are the memorable polemical postcards of local diktats for local people: NO FREE READING; WE NOW SELL GRAVY; the Ikea meatball menu.

On a larger scale, and with more serious intent, there is also an emerging line of documentary publishing that sees a non-ironic engagement in artisan arts, crafts, cooking, etc, which recalls some of the deep south interventions of Jargon Society. In *Small Houses: The Buildings of Tom Browne,* Erica Van Horn captures the retirement project of a local builder, extraordinary miniature houses made of real building materials, in the evidence of photography and text. There is a sense in these recent publications of a counter-offensive, of Coracle playing mainstream publishing at its own game.

sight
is the first
that comes

hearing,
the last
to go

arriving
as the speed
of light

leaving, only
a distant
echo

Notes

1 The heads of the pilchards in this Cornish dish protrude through the pastry crust, so that they appear to be looking skyward.

2 All poems are by Simon Cutts. *Mixed Media Hazard* and 'Ash falls…' are from *Treacle Sandwich Flagpole: Some Poems 1968–1972*, London: Coracle Press, 1975; 'Once their places…,' 'As for the verse…,' *Flower*, and 'Alter the syntax…' from *A New Kind of Tie: Poems 1965–68*, Notts: Tarasque Press, 1972; *le Marché* from *Petits-airs for Margot*, London: Coracle Press, 1986; 'Late starlings…' collected in Simon Cutts, *Pianostool Footnotes*, Cumbria: The Jargon Society, 1982; 'Affections…' from *Leafmould* (with Karl Torok), London: Coracle Press, 1975; *Another Thumbprint: Hedges and Hillsides* from *A Coracle* No 31, 1977; 'Of mundanity…' from 'Palpa,' collected in *Seepages*, Cumbria: The Jargon Society, 1988; 'A goldfish bowl…' and 'Did Ian Hamilton Finlay…' from *Gnomery*, London: Coracle Press, 1983; 'Anything may…' from *Footnotes* to a manual of Shaker Furniture*, London: Coracle Press, 1984; 'Sight is the first…' from *as if it is at all*, Granary Books & Coracle, 2007.

3 'An Interview with Wolfgang Gortschacher' in *Some Forms of Availability: Critical Passages on the Book and Publication by Simon Cutts*. Granary Books / RGAP, 2007.

4 Simon Cutts, introduction to *The Weather House and other works*. Coracle Press for Nottingham: Midland Group Gallery, 1975.

5 This and the following quote from 'An Interview with Wolfgang Gortschacher,' op cit.

6 See correspondence reproduced in 'Homage to Seurat,' in *Some Forms of Availability*, op cit.

7 *Metaphor and Motif.* Nottingham: Midland Group Gallery, 1972.

8 *The Weather House and other works*, ibid.

9 *The Weather House and other works*, ibid.

10 *The Weather House and other works*, ibid.

11 For a detailed appreciation see John Janssen, 'A Coracle Through my Letter-Box: The Invitation Card,' in *The Coracle*. London: Coracle Distribution, 1989.

12 Examined in depth in 'Some Coracle Ephemera,' an arm-wrestling contest between Simon Cutts and Steven Leiber in *Some Forms of Availability*, ibid.

13 Simon Cutts & Colin Sackett, *English Coloured Papers*. Axminster: Colin Sackett, 2008.

14 Duncan Phillips, The Phillips Collection, quoted in *The Coracle in Docking*. Norfolk: Coracle, 1982.

15 On the printing side, there was a casual collective of book artists including Brian Lane, Steve Wheatley, Stephen Duncalf, Les Coleman and others who shared Coracle facilities, and whose technical expertise contributed greatly to Coracle efforts. Colin Sackett and I bridged the gap between this group and a more formal collective, in that we worked full time at Coracle from 1981 and continued for a year or so to publish under our joint imprint Chocolate News Books. From around 1983, Clare Rowe joined Coracle to take care of admin, and Ian Farr and David Gray on editorial, retail and collections. A rota of students from St Martin's, Goldsmiths and Camberwell helped out with collating, print finishing, cleaning, etc.

16 *Coracle Atlantic: An Arena of Art Activity*. Liverpool: Coracle Atlantic Foundation, 1986.

17 A pair of unloved sliding window shutter / display panels taken from the gallery to be recycled in the Coracle garden at Camberwell was found, after a rainstorm dislodged the covering of lining paper, to have been graffiti-painted by Keith Haring. Proceeds helped launch the new Cork Street gallery.

18 Detailed in the critical catalogue résumé by Nancy Kuhl, *The Book Remembers Everything: The Work of Erica Van Horn*. Coracle & Granary Books, 2010.

19 See for example Erica Van Horn, *Reference Files of Envelopes Received*, 3,500 envelopes sewn into 154 books, documented in Nancy Kuhl, ibid.

20 www.coracle.ie/journal/journal.html.

21 Simon Cutts in a note to the author, and possibly elsewhere.

22 From a brief essay on workfortheeyetodo by Simon Cutts, posted on www.thecentreofattention.org/dgwork.html.

23 www.colinsackett.co.uk/bibliography.php.

24 See, for example, Les Coleman, *Dirt & Other Works*, 2009, and the *Certain Trees* catalogue, 2006.

Other references to titles are Coracle publications.

The Norfolk Books 1989–2011

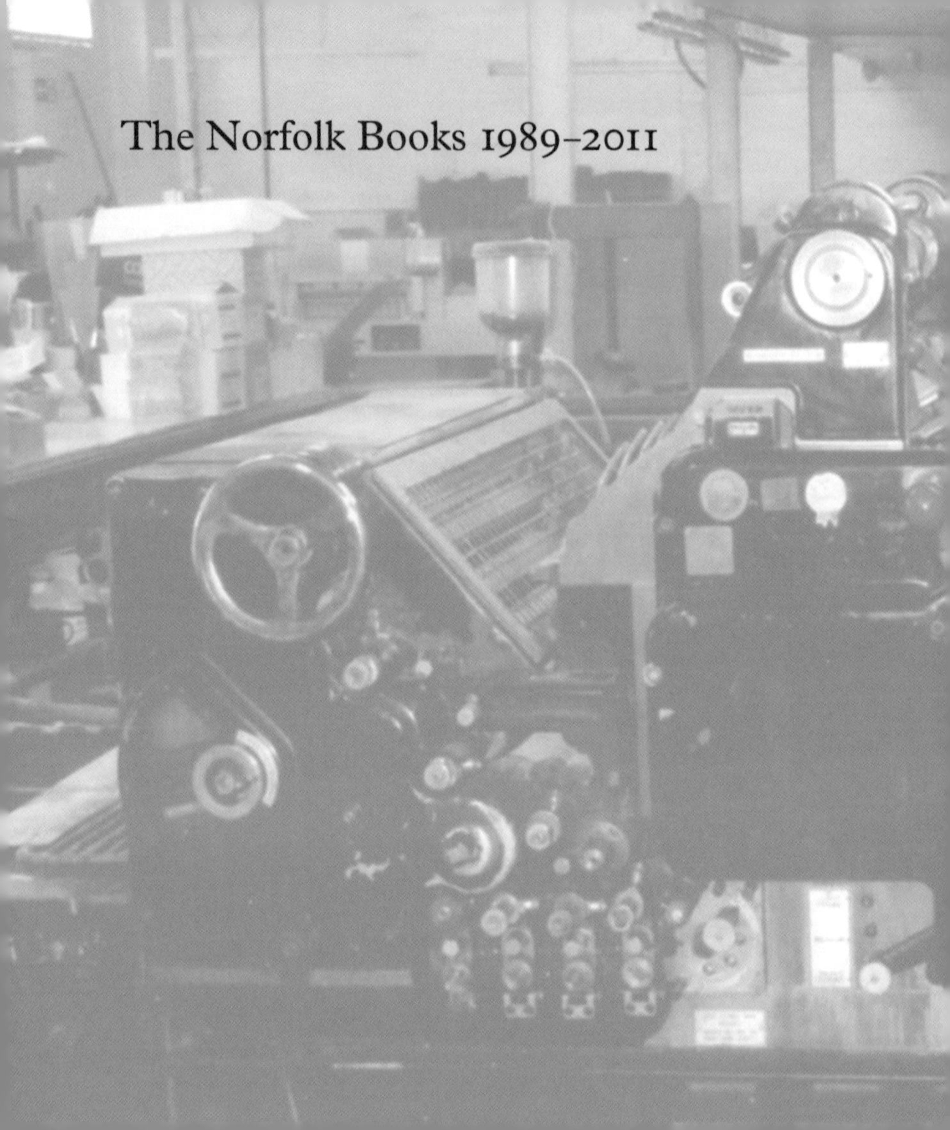

1989

Nine Poems
Simon Cutts
letterpress centre-sewn with wrapper, 24pp in six colours, 328 x 236, 100 numbered copies

Palpa
Simon Cutts
letterpress wire-stitched pamphlet, 16pp, 177 x 127, 300 copies

A New Seed Catalogue
Coracle Press new books
letterpress wire-stitched wrappers

1990

Jewels I Have Loved
Erica Van Horn
letterpress casebound, 28pp in seven colours 186 x 175, 200 signed copies

Sans Signaux
Erica Van Horn & Simon Cutts
letterpress casebound, 24pp in four colours, 261 x 290, 100 copies

1991

Warehouse Catalogue
Coracle Press new books
offset wire-stitched pamphlet, 24pp in 3 colours, 170 x 125, 300 copies

Ducts & Tracts
Stephen Duncalf
offset casebound, 116pp with dust wrapper, 184 x 132, 200 signed copies

1989
Erica Van Horn
offset casebound, 56pp in two colours, 182 x 133, 200 numbered copies

The Sea is Silent
Stuart Mills
letterpress casebound, 24pp in seven colours, 136 x 178, 100 signed copies

1992

Approximate Increments
David Bellingham
offset spiral-bound, 50pp
with 4-colour cover 148 x 200,
250 copies

Notes on Writing & Drinking
Bill Culbert & Simon Cutts
offset, letterpress spiral-bound,
56pp 162 x 113, 183 copies

Inkwell & Paperweight
Simon Cutts
letterpress casebound, 72pp
in ten colours, 154 x 128,
90 numbered copies

Copy
Colin Sackett
offset wire-stitched in plastic,
60pp 170 x 120, 300 copies

Cuckoo
Yoko Terauchi
red pigment and graphite
casebound, 260 x 258,
30 numbered copies

Aglio 6 Olio
Erica Van Horn
& Simon Cutts
xerox & letterpress casebound,
156pp 76 x 76, 200 numbered
copies

Public Art in A Private Time
Vito Acconci
letterpress casebound, 44pp
180 x 135, 300 copies

Antwerp Airport
Erica Van Horn
xerox & paint casebound, 28pp
151 x 129, 35 signed copies

Companions & Menus
Erica Van Horn
& Simon Cutts
multiple processes casebound,
56pp 4-colour offset 181 x 132,
250 numbered copies

Additions & Deletions
Catalogue
offset centre-sewn pamphlet,
16pp with colour photograph
150 x 95, 300 copies

1993

Namenlosen
Colin Sackett
& Simon Cutts
letterpress & offset casebound,
56pp in two colours 260 x 189,
130 numbered copies

Rubber Stamp Mini Printer 1
Simon Cutts
rubber stamps casebound in
slipcase, 76pp 162 x 108,
100 numbered copies

Translated Latrine Inscriptions
Simon Cutts
xerox casebound, 36pp
in two colours 156 x 103,
100 numbered copies

Two Views
Simon Cutts
laser and letterpress casebound,
12pp 301 x 211, 50 numbered
copies

Boy Bell's Book of Envelope Interiors
Erica Van Horn
xerox & letterpress centre-sewn
pamphlet, 24pp with inserts
152 x 146, 50 copies 1st edition

New York High New York Low
Paul Etienne Lincoln
offset with flexidiscs casebound,
300 x 300, 30 numbered copies

1994

Workplace
Don Prince
4-colour offset spiral-bound, 28pp 214 x 100, 500 signed and numbered copies

Stiles & The Pennine Way
Erica Van Horn
offset & letterpress casebound, 4pp in three colours & hand colouring, 362 x 236, 50 copies

Water of Recess
Simon Cutts
& Erica Van Horn
multiple processes boxed, 6pp pamphlet and glass flasks, 35 x 40 x 100, 30 copies

Some Implications of Poetry
workfortheeyetodo
xerox wire-stitched, 16pp 210 x 145, 300 copies

A Windowsill of Books on Landscape
Catalogue
offset wire-stitched with wrapper, 16pp in two colours 127 x 153, 300 copies

Notes on Drinking & Driving
Bill Culbert & Simon Cutts
offset & letterpress wire binding, 90pp in slipcase 148 x 110, 200 copies

Andy Making Holes
Simon Cutts
xerox with additions sewn pamphlet, 16pp 140 x 104, 100 numbered copies

The Waterfalls of New Hampshire in Winter
Simon Cutts
offset plastic wallet binding perfect-bound pad in wallet, 179 x 116, 100 numbered copies

Beyond Border
Don Prince
laser plastic wallet binding, 8pp plastic folder in slipcase 200 x 125, 200 numbered copies

coil / join
Yoko Terauchi
paper, paper-drilling & blind emboss, casebound, 176pp 188 x 188, 22 numbered copies

Envelope Interiors
Erica Van Horn
xerox casebound album & inserts, 288pp with slipcase 154 x 159, 9 copies

Coracle at The Irish Museum of Modern Art
letterpress folded invitation card, 3-fold wallet with 4-fold concertina 108 x 197, 500 copies

Forty Funghi
Erica Van Horn
& Harry Gilonis
offset casebound, 90pp 210 x 150, 200 copies

Identificazione: Italian Lesson 13
Erica Van Horn
letterpress & stamps concertina, 10-panels 80 x 51, 80 x 512, 200 copies, 2 editions

Scraps of An Aborted Collaboration
Erica Van Horn
offset and hand colour Japanese binding, 18pp 113 x 200, 200 numbered copies, 2nd version

Interaction & Overlap
Geoffrey Soar
& David Miller
offset & letterpress wire binding, 40pp 185 x 135, 300 copies

1995

Little Critic 11
Thomas A Clark
letterpress concertina, 4-panel
220 x 155, 300 copies

A Selection of New Books
workfortheeyetodo
xerox wire-stitched, 16pp
210 x 145, 300 copies

An A-Z of Bird Song
John Bevis
offset casebound, 36pp
with dust jacket 204 x 134,
300 numbered copies

lines from walls 1989-1994
Simon Cutts
letterpress casebound
concertina, 8pp 183 x 108,
200 numbered copies

An ode for the recovery of an Olympia Splendid
Simon Cutts
xerox wire binding, 4pp plastic
encapsulation 170 x 120,
70 numbered copies

Rubber Stamp Mini Printer 2
Simon Cutts
rubber stamps casebound,
88pp 171 x 126,
200 numbered copies

Boy Bell's Book of Envelope Interiors
Erica Van Horn
xerox & letterpress centre-sewn
pamphlet, 28pp with inserts
152 x 146, 100 copies
3rd edition

Docking Competitions
Erica van Horn
& Laurie Clark
offset casebound, 48pp in two
colours 150 x 107, 700 copies

Forever Multiples catalogue
workfortheeyetodo
offset wire-stitched, 16pp
155 x 155, 300 copies

1996

Spines & Spirals: The Norfolk Books 1990–96
offset wire binding, 52pp
colour copy cover 107 x 150,
300 copies

A Handful of Stones
Thomas Joshua Cooper
offset & letterpress casebound,
48pp in nine colours 135 x 165,
300 copies

single words for Ian Hamilton Finlay
letterpress casebound, 80pp
in two colours 206 x 115,
196 copies

Gnocchi-Gommi: Italian Lesson 16
Erica Van Horn
letterpress labels on boxed
erasure, 25 x 30 x 68, 40 copies

Gumigas Zimogs
Erica Van Horn
letterpress & stamps wire
binding, 64pp 148 x 115,
200 copies

The A. Goldsworthy Questionnaires
Simon Cutts
letterpress & stamps centre-
sewn, 24pp with wrappers
120 x 100, 200 copies

After Frank O' Hara and Morton Feldman
Erica Van Horn
& Simon Cutts
letterpress centre-sewn, 8pp with wrappers 123 x 110, 200 copies

1999

Little Critic 12
Hamish Maclaren
letterpress wire-stiched pamphlet, 16pp 220 x 155, 300 copies

Only Paranoics Survive
Peter Weibel
letterpress sewn with wrappers, 60pp in 2 colours 180 x 135, 300 copies

14 Blackthorns
Simon Cutts
& Erica Van Horn
letterpress casebound, 60pp in two colours 200 x 110, 200 copies

15 Blackthorns
Erica Van Horn
letterpress print, 420 x 530, 100 numbered copies

Cafe Alt Wien
Simon Cutts
offset sewn with wrappers, 44pp 145 x 110, 200 copies

Some Memorials
Mick Williamson
offset casebound, 48pp case with embossed inlay, 165 x 165, 300 copies

2000

Ex Libris John Janssen: John Janssen at Sixty
letterpress boxed, 33 ex libris labels multiple colours 145 x 125, 125 copies

A History of the Airfields of Lincolnshire II
Simon Cutts
letterpress sewn with wrapper, 32pp 175 x 115, 300 copies

The Pig Poems
Spike Hawkins
& Erica Van Horn
letterpress casebound, 32pp in two colours 300 x 244, 100 numbered copies

2001

I Build My Time
Kurt Schwitters/
Klaus Stadtmuller
letterpress casebound, 108pp
230 x 110, 500 copies

Necklace of Tongues
Alice Maher
4-colour offset & letterpress
casebound, 68pp & tip-ins
200 x 175, 660 numbered
copies

2002

Some Words For Living Locally
Erica Van Horn
letterpress & stamps sewn with
wrappers, 12pp in four colours
147 x 105, 300 numbered and
signed copies

Airmail Envelope Interiors
Erica Van Horn
& Simon Cutts
offset and letterpress sewn
with wrapper, 24pp 115 x 170,
300 numbered copies

Little Critic 16
Les Coleman
offset wire-stitched pamphlet,
16pp 220 x 155, 300 copies

Bedhangings II
Susan Howe
letterpress casebound, 48pp
case with embossed inlay
165 x 130, 300 numbered copies

Fredson Bowers
& The Irish Wolfhound
J. C. C. Mays
4-colour offset casebound,
84pp case with embossed inlay
190 x 140, 500 copies

also
Maud Cotter
letterpress concertina, 4-panel
155 x 105, 500 copies

2003

The Vegetable Plot at L8511
Tim Robinson
4-colour offset & letterpress
print, 445 x 310, 150 numbered
and signed copies

Notional
Katie Holten
offset & stamps casebound,
76pp & tip-ins 170 x 140,
300 numbered copies

2004

Two Peelings 1993-2004
Erica Van Horn
letterpress folded cards in wallet, 2 folded cards 165 x 125, 60 copies

eclogues
Simon Cutts
letterpress casebound, 12pp sewn double gate-folds 175 x 125, 300 copies

sourcebook
Simon Cutts
letterpress & offset sewn with wrappers, 4pp in two colours 150 x 135, 300 copies

An English Dictionary of French Place Names
Simon Cutts
letterpress and offset casebound, 144pp in two colours 220 x 150, 300 copies

other attachments
Maude Cotter
letterpress labels in wallet, 4 labels 225 x 158, 300 copies

2005

(œillets des poétes) *
Simon Cutts
letterpress sewn with wrappers, 8pp 145 x 90, 300 copies

Lemon Red
Cralan Kelder
offset & letterpress sewn with wrappers, 28pp 180 x 135, 300 numbered copies

The Purification of Fagus sylvatica var pendula
Paul Etienne Lincoln
offset casebound, 48pp in two colours 265 x 225, 600 copies

New Potatoes
Helen O'Leary & Paul Chidester
4-colour offset plastic spiral binding, 64pp 140 x 105, 500 copies

2006

Folded Napkins
Erica Van Horn
offset sewn with wrapper, 16pp in two colours 150 x 110, 300 numbered copies

With My Left Hand
Erica Van Horn
letterpress & xerox wire-stitched, 28pp 165 x 133, 300 copies

Led Astray By Language
Jonathan Williams, et al
offset & letterpress sewn with wrapper, 24pp with additions 175 x 135, 300 copies

2007

A little bit of butter
Peter Foynes editor
letterpress & offset casebound,
48pp in seven colours
125 x 175, 500 numbered copies

A Few Cups
Erica Van Horn
letterpress binders box, 9 prints
250 x 250, 25 numbered copies

Little Critic 19
Erica Van Horn
letterpress & offset sewn in
cover, 16pp 210 x 150,
300 copies

2008

8 Old Irish apples
Erica Van Horn
& Simon Cutts
letterpress concertina, 8-panel
90 x 90, 300 copies

Some Alternatives to Flock
John Bevis
offset & letterpress sewn with
wrapper, 48pp 175 x 130,
300 copies

Driven-Out, Ditched & Deserted
Jason Clark
offset & letterpress sewn with
wrapper, 36pp in two colours
175 x 130, 300 copies

Forty Funghi
Harry Gilonis
& Erica Van Horn
offset & letterpress sewn with
wrapper, 96pp 175 x 130,
300 copies

An Album of Interiors
Erica Van Horn
letterpress casebound, 36pp
with tip-ins 235 x 170,
175 numbered copies

Black Bob
Colin Sackett
letterpress casebound, 128pp
175 x 115, 200 copies

short-cuts
Erica Van Horn
& Simon Cutts
letterpress concertina, 8-panel
150 x 90, 300 copies

2009

onglet
Simon Cutts
letterpress casebound, 32pp with cutting & embossing 175 x 125, 125 copies

Poems From A Pioneer Museum
Susan Howe
letterpress binders box, 32 loose cards 130 x 100, 300 numbered and signed copies

2010

picardons et pélardons
Simon Cutts
letterpress sewn with wrapper, 8pp with die-cutting and tip-ins 150 x 100, 300 copies

with or without
Erica Van Horn
laser casebound endpapers with hand-colouring, 180 x 130, 300 copies

Some More Notes on Writing & Drinking
Bill Culbert & Simon Cutts
offset casebound, 60pp with additions and stamps 150 x 110, 175 copies

2011

Mending
Thomas Meyer & Erica Van Horn
letterpress casebound, 24pp with 4 inserts 243 x 184, 80 numbered copies

The Manifestation of the Poem
Simon Cutts
letterpress casebound, 272pp 190 x 127, 100 copies blocked on the spine

Cards and folding cards, posters, announcements & invitations

1982

Coracle Docking, postcard

1990

Franz Erhard Walther, Victoria Miro Gallery, letterpress poster

Broken Lines, Victoria Miro Gallery, letterpress poster

1991

Gallery Resignation 1, Simon Cutts, postcard

Gallery Resignation 2, Simon Cutts, postcard

Skegness Rock, Erica Van Horn, folding card

The Sackner Collection, Simon Cutts, postcard

A. Goldsworthy Productions 1, Simon Cutts, postcard

New York is Death, Sarah Schulman, postcard

I prefer the streams, Simon Cutts, postcard

Happy Picnics, Simon Cutts & Erica Van Horn, folding card

1993

finding a businessman, workfortheeyetodo, postcard

publication for artists, workfortheeyetodo, postcard

A Sunday School Room, workfortheeyetodo, postcard

We now sell gravy, workfortheeyetodo, postcard invitation

A harbour of boat books, cards and prints by Ian Hamilton Finlay, invite, sticker & list

rotatory, Colin Sackett, workfortheeyetodo, postcard invitation

Jean Spencer, workfortheeyetodo, postcard invitation

Address cards, workfortheeyetodo 1993–1996

Lines on the Hoped-for Rejection from The Burnham Market Craft Fair 1993, letterpress poster

Dopple, Simon Cutts & Colin Sackett, postcard invitation

Italian Lessons 11, workfortheeyetodo

1994

Coracle at Kings Lynn Arts Centre, postcard invitation

A Waffle for 1994, folded card in envelope

A Swale Walk, postcard invitation

for the voice, workfortheeyetodo, folded invitation

Other journeys, workfortheeyetodo, invitation

Some Notes on Drinking & Driving, workfortheeyetodo, invitation

Ten Years of Atlas Press, workfortheeyetodo, invitation

Bookworks & Coracle: New Books from London, letterpress poster

for it not to be worth…, Les Coleman, postcard

1995

what's the difference between?, workfortheeyetodo, postcard

what can I give him…?, workfortheeyetodo, postcard

A Black Tie for Artists Books, workfortheeyetodo, postcard

A Day of Readings, workfortheeyetodo, postcard invitation

A Print Event, workfortheeyetodo, invitation

Italian Lessons 14, workfortheeyetodo, postcard

Specialist books by specialists, folding card

An Anecdoted Topography of Chance, workfortheeyetodo, invitation

An Explanation of Light, St Paulinus, folded invitation

Damaged Nature, Gustav Metzger, invitation

1996
No Free Reading, work-fortheeyetodo, postcard & invitation
With Mac & Chain-saw, postcard
Mdm Desvignes Sewing, Simon Cutts, postcard
A. Goldsworthy Productions (snowball), postcard
Italian Lessons 15, work-fortheeyetodo, postcard
Leaving Mon Idée 1982–96, Simon Cutts, postcard
A Cravat for John Janssen, workfortheeyetodo, postcard
The Postcard is A Public Work of Art, WAX366, postcard
Vermeer II, Stewart Home, workfortheeyetodo, postcard invitation
cardworks, workfortheeyetodo, invitation
Five Jug Lamps, Bill Culbert, workfortheeyetodo, postcard invitation

1997
A. Goldsworthy Productions (végetale), postcard
A Trail of Two Bookshops, postcard
A Trail of Two Bookshops, postcard invitation
Envelope Interior Calendars, workfortheeyetodo, invitation
Ten Photographs, Thomas Joshua Cooper, workfortheeye-todo, invitation announcement
The Original Desktop Publisher, Simon Cutts, postcard
the space of the page, Henry Moore Institute, folded invitation
plug card for Mark Pawson, postcard
Change of address card, Coracle, postcard 1998
Coracle Purse, change purse

1999
this postcard is light…, Les Coleman, double-sided postcard
Italian Lessons 17 Mezzo Marito, Erica Van Horn, postcard
A Peanut Butter & Mayo Sandwich, postcard invitation
Café Alt Wien, postcard announcement
14 Blackthorns, postcard announcement
neon poem argon poem, Simon Cutts, folded card in envelope

2000
A History of the Airfields of Lincolnshire, Simon Cutts, postcard invitation

2001
it must be abstract, York City Art Gallery, folded invitation
Harvester / Pat Looby, Temple Bar Gallery, folded invitation

2002
The Money Jar, announcement
3 books, National Library of Ireland, folded invitation

2003
Prolonged Reading, postcard
A Recent History of What's Possible, Katie Holten, announcement
Sale card for MiMo, announcement

2004
for Louis Zukofsky, Harry Gilonis, postcard
Shaker hanger, Erica Van Horn, postcard
Boats, Cots, Punts & Wherries, folded invitation

2005
Living Locally 9—Chaynie, Erica Van Horn, postcard
New Potatoes, Helen O'Leary, postcard
A Bundle of Clothes Pegs, Simon Cutts & Erica Van Horn, folded card

2006
Stilfragen, Erica Van Horn, postcard
Café Ikea Flatpack, Simon Cutts, postcard

River Coracles, postcard
A Celebration of the Life and Work of Stuart Mills, postcard invitation
all his life Mr. S. Mills, Simon Cutts, postcard

2007
Living Locally 10—against mice, Erica Van Horn, postcard

2008
Living Locally 15, Erica Van Horn, postcard
Certain Trees, card announcement
Rosemary, Erica Van Horn, postcard
They're Giving Good, Erica Van Horn, postcard

2010
The Golden Bough, Katie Holten, announcement

2011
from The Journal, Erica Van Horn, folded booklet cover

Bibliography

The Open and Closed Book, R. C. Kenedy. Victoria & Albert Museum, 1979

The Artist Publisher. Coracle for the Crafts Council of Great Britain, 1986

The Coracle: Coracle Press Gallery 1975–1989. Yale Center for British Art, 1989

Work and Turn: Artists' Bookworks from the United Kingdom. Open Editions, 1992

Interaction & Overlap: from the Little Magazine and Small Press Collection at University College, ed. Geoffrey Soar and David Miller. workfortheyetodo, 1994

The Space of the Page: Sequence, Continuity & Material, ed. John Janssen, Erica Van Horn and Simon Cutts. Henry Moore Institute, 1997

Repetivity: platforms and approaches to publishing. RGAP, Derby, 2000

The Presence of Landscape: printed objects, cards and books by Coracle 1975–2000. Centre Culturel Jean Gagnant, Limoges, 2000

Brian Lane: The Printed Performance. RGAP, Derby, 2001

Englshpublshing: Colin Sackett, Writing and readings 1991–2002. Coracle et al, 2004

Vinyl: project for installation. Coracle for Cork 2005

Certain Trees: the constructed book, poem and object 1964–2006. CDLA, St Yrieix la Perche, 2006

Some Forms of Availability: Critical Passages on the Book and Publication, Simon Cutts. Granary Books and RGAP, 2007

The Book Remembers Everything: The Work of Erica Van Horn, Nancy Kuhl. Granary Books and Coracle, 2010

List of Illustrations

ARTS COUNCIL ENGLAND
LOTTERY FUNDED

The Elephant Trust

Norfolk County Council

The Henry Moore Foundation